We Just Got
On With It

We Just Got On With It

CHANGES BEFORE, DURING AND AFTER THE SECOND WORLD WAR IN NORTHERN IRELAND

With the compliments of

Doreen McBride

Doreen McBride

First published 2022

The History Press
97 St George's Place, Cheltenham,
Gloucestershire, GL50 3QB
www.thehistorypress.co.uk

British Library Cataloguing in Publication Data.
A catalogue record for this book is available from the British Library.

ISBN 978 0 7509 9878 9

Typesetting and origination by The History Press
Printed and bound in Great Britain by TJ Books Limited, Padstow, Cornwall.

MIX
Paper from
responsible sources
FSC® C013056

Trees for Life

Contents

Acknowledgements

I'd like to thank everyone who contributed to this book. It began during a discussion between good friends, who are members of local historical societies, namely Florence Chambers, Bridie Gallagher, Patrick Greer, Pat McGuigan and Bridgeen Rutherford. They realised that memories of how we lived in the recent past are in the process of disappearing and should be recorded. I was worried because editing somebody else's work can lead to controversy. I didn't find that. I found nothing but helpful attitudes and sensible suggestions, and I feel I've made good friends.

Special thanks are due to my husband, George, who not only made helpful suggestions but contributed his memories, and to another contributor, my cousin Vernon Finlay, who is a constant source of encouragement and inspiration. He read the manuscript, corrected many of my mistakes and made helpful suggestions.

Thanks are due to the Belfast Central Library's Reference Library, Armagh Museum and the Linen Hall Library. They could not have been more helpful. As far as my personal memories are concerned, I'd like to thank my extended family, my sister Eileen Finlay and her husband Alan Finlay, cousins Alan Lyle and Rhonda Devonport, for jogging my memory by joining me in old-age reminiscences sessions. I enjoyed the craic and the happy memories of grandparents, Sam and Sarah Finlay, Norman and Lizzie Henry, great-granny ('old') Martha Henry, Auntie Teenie, Old Jim, Big Jim and Wee Jim, Auntie Carrie and Uncle Willie Husband and Uncle Norman Finlay and last but not least my parents, Bill and Anne Henry. My father was a keen semi-professional photographer who took many of the images.

Thanks are also due to Belfast Zoo for permission to use photos of the baby elephant, to the *Belfast Telegraph* for permission to use photograph of a bus passing Stormont, Beryl Higgins and to North Belfast Historical Society and the *Banbridge Chronicle*, contributors, and others, who supplied photographs.

I appreciate information gleaned from old friends and acquaintances including Davis Martin, Judith Neely, Arthur Wallace, Florence Creighton, Neil Spiers, Linda Patterson, Mr Magill, Anne McMaster, Alan Finlay, Ella Brown, Alan Byrne, Norah Bates, George Close, Raymond Turner, Bobby Foster, The Spectrum Centre, The Strand Arts Centre, Millisle Primary School, Orangefield Primary School and Nigel McKelvey.

Thanks are also due to old friends who are no longer with us: Dr Bill Crawford, Ernest and Marjorie Scott, Edith Chaplin, Francie Shaw, my cousin Christine Pickin, Roy Leinster, Jim Lyle, Billy Simpson, Dr Vivien Gotto, Joan Gafney, Dolly Skuce, Mrs Mackay, Tommy McMaster and John Campbell.

Invaluable help has been given by Rosie Hickey and the Strand Arts Centre, the staff of the *Banbridge Chronicle*, especially François Vincent, who took local information I passed him and turned it into a series of newspaper articles. He also delved through the paper's archives for photographs and contributed to this book. David Hume, who writes for the *East Antrim Times*, asked his readers for information regarding the war and that resulted in contributions from that area.

I am also very grateful to my editors Nicola Guy and Ele Craker, who are a constant source of encouragement, advice and patience.

List of Contributors

Some contributors do not wish to be fully named for personal reasons.

George Beattie, Thomas Black, Bob Beggs, Larry Breen, Marjorie Burnett, Florence Chambers, Garnet Chambers, Jimmy (Jimbo) Conway, Jason Diamond, Duncan Mundo Jr, Frankie Elliott, Jane Elliott (née Burns), Bobby Evans, Joe Evans, Margaret Farnsworth (née Cairns), Vernon Finlay, Eileen Finlay, Joe Furphy, Bill Graham, the late Paddy Gillespie, Margaret Graham, Patrick Greer, Bill Gordon, Adrian Hack, Evelyn Hannah, Rosie Hickey, William Hillis, Jay, Margaret Jones, John Kelly, John Logan, Alan Lyle, Pat McGuigan, Doreen McBride, George McBride, Noel McBride, Eileen McCormick, Marian McDowell, Bridie McGillion, Sean McIlroy, Marianne Nelson, George Nesbitt, Lisa Rawlins, Bridgeen Rutherford, Heather Taylor, Jim Taylor, François Vincent, Billy W., Charles Warmington, George Wilson, Marion Wilson.

Introduction

This book is the result of what could be loosely called an OAP reminiscence session, except one of us is only in his fifties! We are friends who belong to Historical Societies in Northern Ireland. Bridgeen Rutherford is Chair of New Buildings & District Archaeological and Historical Society in County Londonderry, Patrick Greer is Chair of West Belfast Historical Society, Florence Chambers is the Secretary of Banbridge Historical Society. I'm Press Officer of Banbridge Historical Society. Last but not least there's Pat MacGuigan, whose fingers are in so many pies he'd prefer not to be classified as belonging to a particular society. We are busy people who meet irregularly, for a meal and a bit of craic, in a pub in Belfast.

It was at one of these meetings that the subject of the Second World War came up. President Roosevelt is on record saying the Allies could not have won the Second World War without the contribution made by Northern Ireland. We started chatting.

Because we live, in Northern Irish terms, so far apart, we either had personal memories, or memories passed down from parents and grandparents from different parts of the province. Our stories ranged from being hilariously funny to absolutely tragic. We looked at each other and agreed that when our generation snuffs it those memories will disappear. That would be a shame and they should be recorded. 'You write it!' they said. I protested, 'I can only write about my memories! I can't write about yours. You'd have to do that yourselves.' They agreed.

Florence looked thoughtful. 'We're all members of historical societies, the book would be improved if we collected memories from members as well. It would be more complete.' I groaned, 'That's a nightmare.'

Bridgeen agreed. 'You're right. We'd get lots of accounts about how everyone used newspapers instead of toilet rolls and that would be boring.'

Mac piped up, 'Doreen could act as editor. She could tell History Press about it and see what they think.'

I agreed. 'The book should be written but – and it is a big BUT – I don't think I want to edit it because people could be highly offended by my actions.'

'No problem!' said Patrick. 'We'll explain what you're doing. Arrange the book in chapters and make sure everyone who contributes gets a mention, and make sure it's not all doom and destruction. You're sure to find a lot of humour! (I did!) We want a complete picture of life before, during and after the war in Northern Ireland.'

I went home and wondered if the *Banbridge Chronicle* would be interested in local war stories, so I had a chat with François Vincent, a journalist on the paper. He was very supportive and suggested publishing a series on whatever local information turned up. I also contacted Nicola Guy, a commissioning editor at The History Press, and found her, as usual, a supportive, helpful mine of information and encouragement.

I was born in East Belfast just before the Second World War and have the type of memory that is both a blessing and a curse. I have a very good memory for conversations, places and how I felt at a particular time, but my memory is abysmal for names and faces. That can be very embarrassing! The good thing is that if my memory is jogged I can usually redeem myself by saying, 'Oh! I'm sorry. I remember now. We talked about …!' I remember life during the war very clearly and am delighted to share my recollections, along with those of friends and acquaintances, because the old lifestyle has disappeared.

This is not meant to be an academic exercise. It's simply a record of the day-to-day lifestyle of people in Northern Ireland, their contribution to the war effort and the changes that began to occur after the war. I am sure the lack of facilities and the poverty described were common throughout the British Isles and were not confined to Northern Ireland. People appear to have been happy. Time and again those who are now in their nineties said, 'We were poor, but we didn't know it so we were happy.'

Introduction

Originally we thought we'd stop recording after the Festival of Britain in 1951, but we discovered there were no big changes until television became a common possession in the 1950s, the advent of supermarkets and the pill in the early '60s, so we extended our time line.

I apologise as I feel this book is incomplete. The time lapse, and the fact that it is recording personal memories, means there are notable omissions from such organisations as Harland and Wolff, Short Brothers, James Mackie and Sons, and others, and the magnificent contribution they made to the war effort.

Patrick Greer has placed our work in context.

1

Life in Northern Ireland Before and During the Second World War

Politics and Attitudes

Northern Ireland was established in 1921 when six of the nine counties of the Province of Ulster choose to retain British rule, while the other twenty-six counties opted to become a separate entity ruled from Dublin but remaining within the British Commonwealth and known at that time as the Irish Free State. After the war, the Irish Free State decided to break all ties with Britain. It opted out of the Commonwealth and became known as the Republic of Ireland. Its constitutional name is Ireland.

It is difficult to know how to refer to that part of Ireland that remains connected with Britain. To say 'Ulster' is incorrect. Ulster has nine counties and three of the them, Monaghan, Cavan and Donegal, are in the Republic. The six that voted to remain in the United Kingdom are referred to as Northern Ireland. That's not strictly true either because parts of County Donegal are further north than the rest of Northern Ireland. For the purpose of simplicity I'm going to refer to that small part of Ireland that remains under British rule as either Northern Ireland or the 'North' and the Republic of Ireland as the 'South'.

Wounds caused by the Easter Rising, the subsequent Civil War in the South, and terrorist attacks in the North were still raw. Great wrongs were done on both sides of the political divide. Many people tended to be suspicious of the 'other sort'. It was something not apparent in my family, although my mother did say, 'Doreen, Catholics are perfectly nice people. I'd like you to be friends with them, but you mustn't think of marrying one because they'll make you change your religion.' That was true at the time. The Roman Catholic Church in Ireland (I don't know what happened elsewhere) refused to allow a Catholic to marry a Protestant unless the Protestant underwent instruction in the Catholic faith and accepted it as the only true religion. Religion was an important part of life. Practically everyone dressed up in their best clothes, wearing good shoes, with the women wearing a hat and gloves and the men wore a tie, shirt and suit going to church on Sunday. Catholic attitudes to marriage softened so for some time Protestants did not have to change religion, but had to promise any children would be brought up as Catholics. Today there is no problem. I have many friends and acquaintances who are in mixed marriages, and churches have lost the tight hold they once had.

Many Protestants were forced out of the South during the Civil War, leading to great feelings of bitterness. When I taught in Wallace High School the late **Fred Maunsell** was Head of the Classics Department. Fred's father was a policeman, stationed in County Cork during the Civil War. Fred said, 'My father was in a terrible state one evening when he came off duty. He said he'd got a tip-off that the IRA intended to burn us out that night. We gathered whatever valuables we could put in our pockets, climbed up a large tree and waited in fear and trembling. The IRA arrived about one o'clock, set the house and outhouses on fire and disappeared. I was so frightened I shook so much I thought I might fall out of the tree.' At dawn the family climbed down, walked through the fields and headed north. Protestants comprised 40 per cent of the population of Dundalk (a border town) prior to partition. Today it is 2 per cent. In contrast, the Catholic population in the North of Ireland has gone up. At the 2011 census it was 49 per cent Catholic and 51 per cent Protestant.

This book has been produced with the help of close friends of differing beliefs, who are genuinely fond of each other and who have been working to collect cross-community memories. I feel privileged to have been involved.

Industrialisation

(also see Chapter 2)

Belfast was a thriving industrial city with great pride in itself. Its citizens boasted, 'Belfast has the world's largest single shipyard, Harland and Wolff, and the world's largest rope works.' (It was surrounded by a huge wall on the junction of the Albert Bridge and the Newtownards Road.) Towering ships, in the course of construction, dominated terraced houses. People living in Belfast knew the names of all the ships in the yard and were interested in their fate. I remember my mother and her best friend, who I knew as Auntie Sally (**Sally Anderson**), crying because HMS *Eagle* had been sunk.

Harland and Wolff held the British record for ship production. It built 140 warships, 123 merchant ships and more than 500 tanks, and became a key target for the Luftwaffe.

Harland and Wolff shipyard in 1941 after the Blitz. (Photograph printed with kind permission of East Belfast Historical Society)

Medical Services

Before the introduction of the National Health Service (1944 in England, 1947 in Northern Ireland) people had to pay for medical services. Many were living on the breadline. They couldn't afford a doctor's fee, so they didn't send for one until it was too late. Most people self-medicated, relying on herbs to cure disease.

Family doctors were invariably male. The doctor had consulting rooms in his home and his wife acted as secretary. He did everything – syringed wax out of ears, dressed wounds, sounded chests, took samples of blood, the lot. There was no system of booking appointments. You went into the doctor's invariably crowded waiting room, sat down on one of the hard Bentwood chairs and waited your turn. Eventually the doctor came and escorted you to his consulting room. If you needed a house call you phoned the doctor, or what was more likely, went and knocked on his door and he came to you. Home births were the norm. Babies were delivered by the doctor and husbands weren't allowed to be present at the birth. If the woman was comfortably well off she had a midwife in attendance as well as her doctor. New mothers were supposed to stay in bed, and be waited on hand and foot, for two weeks after the birth while the midwife undertook running the house. If there was no other help she cooked and cleaned as well as cared for the 'patient' and her baby. Many mothers couldn't afford to go near a doctor until towards the end of their pregnancy and infant mortality was consequently high.

Hospitals smelt of disinfectant. They had large single-sex wards. Each bed had curtains that could be pulled round to give an illusion of privacy. There were usually two private rooms at the entrance of the ward for individual patients who were seriously ill. Fresh air was thought to be good for patients, so wards in many hospitals, such as Belfast's Royal Victoria, had a wide balcony with French doors so patients could be wheeled out into the fresh air. Visiting hours were strictly regulated and a matron was in charge. She was an intimidating force, ruling with a rod of iron and making sure the hospital stank of cleanliness! She inspected nurses' uniforms, made sure beds were made up with immaculate hospital corners, and she was known to barge (scold) doctors, patients and nurses alike.

Cowan Heron Hospital. (Sourced by François Vincent from *Banbridge Chronicle* archives)

Thomas Black's mother died in 1947 in the Cowan Heron Hospital, Dromore. She was 46 years of age. Thomas was never told either why, or exactly when she died. There were no phones and he doesn't even know how his father heard of her death. When Thomas realised his mother wasn't coming home he took comfort from the following verse:

> Isn't it strange the one we liked,
> And the ones we loved the best,
> Are just the ones that God loves too
> And takes them home to rest.

Thomas has often wondered why his mother died. Penicillin was the first antibiotic to be freely available. It didn't come into general use until towards the end of the 1940s and diseases such as scarlet fever and diphtheria were killers. The only vaccination available was against smallpox, a disease that has since been eradicated, so babies weren't protected against disease the way they are today.

The introduction of the NHS changed attitudes and habits. Some people, when they hadn't to pay their doctors, took advantage of the system. Thomas remembers attending his doctor, Dr Sterling, in Dromore. Thomas says, 'After the introduction of the NHS two Dromore women used to go to the doctors every day. They must have enjoyed the waiting room craic because there wasn't a thing wrong with them! One day one of the women was absent. The next day Dr Sterling asked, "Where were you yesterday?" She replied, "I couldn't come. I wasn't well!"'

The late **Angela Dillon**, past President of Banbridge Historical Society, had scarlet fever as a child. She recorded her experiences of being a patient in Spelga Fever Hospital during the 1940s. (The hospital was in the grounds of Banbridge's workhouse. The site now contains Banbridge Healthcare Centre.)

Angela recorded: 'On admission you were given a good scrub in a bath containing Jeyes Fluid, which made your skin smart. Patients with diphtheria were separated from those with scarlet fever, and most diphtheria patients died.

'Once they started to recover, children with scarlet fever were allowed out into the fresh air to play. We used to stand in the playground and goggle as tiny white coffins were carried across from the diphtheria wards to the morgue. That didn't strike us as having any particular significance. You never thought that you were going to die and you didn't know who was in the coffin. My Aunt Minnie came to a ditch at the edge of the hospital grounds and threw sweets to me.'

I have my own unhappy memories of being in hospital in Belfast. I was very young when I was rushed, with suspected scarlet fever, to Haypark Fever Hospital on the Ormeau Road. My mother was allowed to come with me in the ambulance. A nurse lifted me and told my mother she'd give me a bath. Mum said I'd had a bath earlier in the night. Nurse said a rule was a rule and I would be bathed. Mum was sent away. Nurse was very rough. She dumped me in lukewarm water containing Jeyes Fluid and scrubbed me with carbolic soap. My skin smarted, she hurt me and I screamed. She said, "I'll give you something to cry about!" and gave me a good hiding!

After my bath I was taken into a large ward. It was completely empty apart from rows of cots. Nurse threw me into one and left me alone. I thought the ward was full of ghosts. I was terrified!

My parents visited every day. They weren't allowed into the ward but could watch me through a small window set in the closed door. Nurse told them if I saw them I would be upset and want to go home! I thought I'd been abandoned, lost my appetite, refused to eat and became so run down one of the glands under my left arm went septic. Nurse was cross and scolded as she dressed it. She said it was my own fault because I wouldn't eat! I was frightened because I thought my arm would fall off, but didn't dare say so.

My parents said afterwards it broke their hearts watching me cry my heart out so they brought me my favourite toy, a cuddly pink rabbit with well-sucked bald ears. I wasn't allowed to bring it home in case it carried infection. It was burnt and I mourned its loss. Afterwards my parents said if they'd been told what would happen they'd never have brought it to the hospital.

Eventually an older girl, called Patsy, was put into the cot beside me. She'd had scarlet fever and was waiting to be discharged. When nurse left the room Patsy looked at me and said, "You poor wee soul. You need a hug." She climbed out of her cot and into mine and cuddled me. I snuggled up to her and was comforted. Next morning nurse found us fast asleep in each other's arms. She smacked Patsy for climbing out of her cot and thumped me for allowing her into my bed! Unfortunately Patsy must have had nits so I went home with head lice, but I'm still grateful for the comfort she gave me. It was very difficult to cure head lice in those days. Mum was told to repeatedly wash my hair with Dettol and make me sit with my head bent over a spread-out newspaper while she combed my hair with a fine-toothed nit comb. The nits were knocked onto the newspaper and it was rolled up and burnt, but some eggs survived and the process had to be repeated.

A nurse, known as the 'nit nurse', travelled around schools inspecting children's hair and sending those unfortunates harbouring nits home. She also inspected ears. We stood in miserable lines spitting on our handkerchiefs, feverishly using them to hoke down our ears to make sure they were clean. A school doctor also did the rounds. He decided I looked pale and needed ultraviolet sun ray treatment, so I was made to attend a clinic in Cherryville Street once a week. I had to get out of school, walk to the clinic and join others, stripped to the waist, wearing dark goggles, sitting cross-legged on the floor while ultraviolet lamps shone on us. As far as I remember we were 'cooked' for twenty minutes back and front. A very nice woman supervised us and we played games such as "I spy". I hated it. It's ironic that today we use sunscreen to protect us from ultraviolet rays!

It was a long walk from Orangefield Primary School to Cherryville Street Clinic. Once I was very frightened because a large dog followed me as I walked alone up Orby Drive. Normally I like dogs but I thought this one might think I smelt cooked and might want to eat me!'

Attitudes to Women

Before the war the only jobs available to women were working in a mill or factory, shop assistant, secretarial work, teaching, domestic service, or nursing. There were very few women doctors. Girls from wealthy homes used to 'stay at home and help Mummy' until they managed to find a husband. My father did well in business, so in my late teens we moved to Belfast's Malone Road, an upmarket area. By that time I was determined to go to university. Some of the other girls there sneered at me, 'You must be very clever!' Being 'clever' was considered a disadvantage in the marriage market! Marriage was considered a lifetime career and divorce a disgrace. Unfortunate women had no means of support apart from whatever money their husbands gave them, so if a woman's husband was unfaithful, or abusive, she just had to grin and bear it. There were no state pensions and help for the unemployed was practically non-existent. The dreaded workhouse, also known as the poorhouse, was still in existence.

It was usual for women to stop working on marriage and most definitely after the birth of your first child. That attitude persisted until well into the 1960s. I caused a split in the staff room of Wallace High School in Lisburn by returning to work after the birth of my daughter in the 1960s. I felt I hadn't spent years studying for a degree to sit at home scratching! In those days women were allocated twelve weeks' maternity leave, six weeks before the birth and six weeks after it. There was no provision for paternity leave and men were not allowed to be present at the birth. My very welcome daughter was born in April 1964 and I went back to work in May. I was extremely lucky because the Headmaster of Wallace High School, **T.C.C. Adams**, was a caring individual. He called me into his office on my first day back, and I entered in fear and trembling. I suspected he might enquire if I thought I could do my job now I was a mother! To my surprise he said, 'My wife has had six children. I know you're not going to admit it, but having a baby takes a lot out of you. I've been looking at your timetable. You have A Level classes every afternoon and a couple of first-formers. I want you to go home every day at two o'clock until the end of term. My wife used to teach biology. She'll cover your first-formers out of love of teaching. In September I expect you to work hard!' His attitude was very unusual!

Courtship

Joe Furphy describes a typical courtship of the time. He recalls, 'When I became organist in Hill Street Presbyterian Church, Lurgan, I discovered there was something about the controls of the organ that I did not quite understand and enquired if there was anyone in the choir who could help. I was told a young lady called Margaret knew the workings of the instrument and, yes, she helped me out of my problem. However, there was something about her approach that I did not like and I thought to myself, "That's one girl I won't have any dealings with." Much later I discovered that I had had a similar same effect on her! Thanks to our initial reaction to each other, our relationship developed at even slower pace than most.

Joe Furphy. (Photograph by David Murray, printed with kind permission of joe Furph)

'It was customary for Hill Street Presbyterian Choir to have a dinner and entertainment approaching Christmas and one of the altos, Winnie Cranston, made a suggestion that perhaps Margaret and I could play piano duets at it.

'We reluctantly agreed. However, there was a certain amount of shared pleasure at this musical activity. Winnie persuaded us to continue, kindly making her piano available to us for practice. Something else developed – Margaret lived on the Banbridge Road and I began to give her a lift after our Sunday evening service. Discovering that neither of us had a social partner of the opposite gender, I plucked up courage and suggested a date.

'She agreed and we had our first evening out – appropriately – on St Valentine's Day.

'Single and eligible though we both were, these were very different times – particularly within church settings – and our romance started as a top-secret liaison as we felt it could lead to comments – frivolous and otherwise – in the choir. However, one evening, the Lurgan Harmonic Girls' Choir, including six or seven members of the church choir – one of whom being Margaret – performed at Belfast Music Festival. I was there in another choir, and after the competition Margaret and I went off for a cup of coffee. On the way back to the car, we met our Hill Street friends and our cover was blown!

'The following summer we were both teachers, so we had the opportunity to spend time together during the holidays. We made use of our free days to visit many beautiful places. We also enjoyed two overnight stays in Dublin in a guesthouse – in separate bedrooms.

'I mention this because societal norms have changed beyond recognition since the 1950s and '60s. Courtship was a much slower process than it appears to be today. A girl was considered a "disgrace" to herself and to her family if she became pregnant outside marriage. She could be forced to marry the father of her unborn child. If the man concerned refused to acknowledge paternity her parents would, in all probability, turn her out of the house. The only thing she could do then was to turn to one of the terrible homes for unmarried mothers, run by the churches – and, as we all know, their notorious legacy has been all over the news. There she would have been harshly treated, forced to work hard doing something like laundry, and been forced to give her baby up for adoption.

'We had actually been more discreet than we had realised, and on the evening we approached our minister to make the wedding arrangements, he confessed he was completely unaware of our relationship!

'We tied the knot in Moira Presbyterian Church. After getting married, we spent our honeymoon on the Isle of Skye.

'Sadly our marriage came to end much too early with Margaret's death through illness in 2010.

'By today's standards, our life journey could almost be described as an "alternative lifestyle" in that Margaret and I married and actually stayed married until death did us part.'

Law and Order

Northern Ireland's police force was called the Royal Ulster Constabulary (RUC). They were armed from their inception due to the threat from the Irish Republican Army (IRA).

Locals called them the 'polis' and they were treated with respect bordering on fear. Children used to whisper to each other, when they saw a policeman, 'There's the polis', and disappear indoors. The crime rate was low, murder was unknown. We told each other, 'You mustn't kill anyone, or you'll be hung!'. On 12 November 1952, Judge Curran's 19-year-old daughter Patricia, a student at Queen's University Belfast, was murdered. Her body was found in the driveway of her home, Glen House, Whiteabbey, County Antrim. She had been stabbed thirty-seven times. Everyone was shocked! Such things didn't happen in Northern Ireland. It was a great scandal, the subject of conversation for months afterwards. Imagine that! A murder! Here!

Jim Taylor was born in Conway Street on Belfast's Shankill Road. He writes: 'Not all visitors to our street were welcome! Pig Manelly was a very large policeman (back then we never knew the significance of Pig, we just knew everyone called him that). We would be playing football in the street, he would come pedalling around the corner on his black BSA police bike, jump off, chase us and give us a clip around the ear. We didn't tell our parents as we would have got another clip.'

Jim Taylor. (Photograph printed with kind permission of Jim Taylor)

Housing

Housing for industrial workers was poor, although the city escaped most of the notorious back-to-back slums once common in England. Blue-collar workers lived in small terraced houses of the type known as a 'two-up two-down', meaning it had two rooms downstairs and two bedrooms upstairs. Their walls were built of single brick and their construction was so shoddy that if one was hit by a bomb it caused a domino effect, making the whole row liable to fall down. They didn't have bathrooms, just an outside toilet in the yard and a cold water tap over the jawbox (Belfast sink) in the scullery, an inner room that passed for a kitchen. Families took great pride in their homes and wives, or daughters, scrubbed the outside step every day.

White-collar workers lived in well-built semi-detached houses with bathrooms and gardens in the suburbs, such as those on the Castlereagh and Cregagh Roads.

I lived in a semi-detached house in Orby Parade off the Castlereagh Road, Belfast. My father, **William Lyle Henry**, was a white-collar worker. It was a typical 1930s semi-detached, very different from the terrace houses that housed mill workers. My parents bought it off-plan, it was finished in February

Large terraced houses in South Belfast.

1938 and I was born in it. It had cavity walls everywhere except the one at the back of the kitchen. Dad painted it with waterproof paint so it wasn't damp. We thought it was very posh because it had two toilets, one built into the house and opening into the back garden and one upstairs beside the bathroom. Neither toilet had a wash-hand basin. The bathroom contained a built-in bath, a wash-hand basin and beside the bath there was a large dual-purpose box, with a cork top, that Granda had made. It was used as a seat and a soiled linen basket. Dad had a small cabinet, with a built-in mirror, above the wash-hand basin. A towel rail was screwed into the door and we all used the same towel.

Mill and factory owners lived in large houses on the Antrim Road, the Malone Road or on what is known as the 'Gold Coast', that's the road between Belfast and Bangor. There was a regular, reliable train service that gave easy access to the city. Most of these houses had extensive gardens, bathrooms, kitchens and the occasional one even had central heating, a fridge and a washing machine, things that were very expensive and largely unknown.

My father's aunt, **Christine Lyle (née Henry)**, known as **Teenie**, lived in Morpeth Street off the Shankill Road in West Belfast. It was a typical two-up two-down.

Aunt Teenie was fun. I loved visiting her and am in a good position to describe life in a blue-collar worker's home during and immediately after the war. What I have to say is also applicable to mill workers' houses throughout the province. Repeatedly people have told me, 'We were poor, but we didn't know it, so we were happy. We didn't know what we were missing.' There was no television, the 'pictures', now called movies, showed a world of make believe, sheer escapism

(Auntie) Teenie Lyle and grandchild Jim Lyle. (Photograph printed with kind permission of Alan Lyle)

as far as we were concerned. We didn't take the luxury depicted seriously. The Second World War, dreadful though it was, didn't make an appreciable difference to attitudes and lifestyle. The advent of Social Security, television and the pill between the end of the war and the 1960s did.

Life in Morpeth Street was typical of the period. It was a very supportive community. On warm summer evenings the women came out of their houses and sat on stools, or chairs, beside their front doors. There they knit, sewed or mended while chatting to each other. Anyone walking up the street received a friendly greeting. Children played on the street and relatives lived close by. Teenie and her family were typical. She lived with her husband, **Old Jim Lyle**, her daughter **Betty Lyle** and her mother, **Martha Henry**, while her son, known as **Big Jim Lyle** to differentiate him from his father, and his son **Wee Jim Lyle**, lived further down the street with his wife **Lily**, Wee Jim and his second son, **Alan Lyle**, who was born in 1948. My grandmother, **Lizzie Henry**, lived in the corner shop at the end of the street with her husband **Norman Henry** before buying a small semi-detached house, 1 Glencairn Crescent, Ballygomartin Road. She was the first family member to buy a house. The vast majority of people lived in rented accommodation.

Granny and Granda Henry (Photograph by Bill Henry)

As far as I know, the roof spaces in Morpeth Street weren't connected. In Dee Street, on the Newtownards Road in East Belfast, the houses were built as one continuous unit with internal walls separating the houses and a continuous roof space. Anyone being chased by the police could disappear in the door of one house, climb the stairs and find access to the roof space, run across it and come out a door at other end of the street when the coast was clear!

Norman, like most of the men in his district, worked in Harland and Wolff's Shipyard. He drove a crane. Old Jim was a butcher. He was a very hard worker who had originally owned three butcher's shops in the area but had been burnt out by the IRA during the troubles in 1921. He swore like a trooper when he remembered but held no grudge against Catholics in general, just the b★★★★y f★★★★★s who'd put him out of business!

Morpeth Street was off Northumberland Street, which connects the Shankill and the Falls. Its residents could remember rebels shooting up and down the road at the time of partition. As a result the Shankill became predominantly Protestant and the Falls Catholic. Attitudes of residents on either side of the divide were mixed. The vast majority simply wanted to live in peace with their neighbours and secretly maintained their old pre-Trouble friendships. Auntie Teenie had a very close friend who lived on the Falls. They supported each other through thick and thin, to the extent of giving each other money in times of need. After the 'Troubles' they could no longer meet openly in their respective neighbourhoods because of the existence of the occasional sectarian hothead. They met, in central Belfast, every Wednesday afternoon for afternoon tea in The Carleton, and continued to do so until the 1970s when Teenie's friend died.

Teenie's house living room was tiny. It was heated by a coal fire on the wall furthest away from the front door and at right angles to it. The room was lit by a small window near the door and had two small upholstered chairs that matched the small two-seater sofa occupying the wall opposite the front door. It was beside a door leading into the scullery.

The scullery took the place of today's kitchen. It was very sparsely furnished with a gas stove, and a jawbox supplied with cold water from a tap. There was a cupboard to the right of the door housing all kitchen utensils, a pine-scrubbed table under the window and a back door leading to the yard.

Jim Taylor, who was born in 1945, writes, 'I was born in 165 Conway Street in my grandmother's house. It had two bedrooms. My grandmother

Johnny the knocker-upper.
(Printed with kind permission
of Jim Taylor Jim Taylor)

and her daughter, Betty, slept in one room. My mum, dad and I slept in the other at night. My uncle Willie, who worked night shift, slept in our bedroom during the day. When I was one year old we moved around the corner to 34 Fourth Street.

'The area where I lived off the Shankill Road in Belfast was surrounded by factories and mills and every morning the hooters would go off to let people know it was time for work. The factory's gates would close exactly at 8 a.m.; if you were late you were locked out without pay.

'Alarm clocks were rare and John the knocker-upper was hired to go around the streets with two large bamboo canes joined together. John would come at an agreed time and use the bamboo canes to knock on the upstairs bedroom windows.

'The houses were small. Each side of the streets had about thirty houses and most workers slept in the upstairs front rooms so they could hear the knocker-upper.

'When I was growing up the air raid shelters, built during the war, were still there with brick walls and a large concrete roof, which we climbed on. They were disgusting because children and drunks weaving their way home on a Friday night often used them as urinals.'

Sewage Disposal and Water Supply

(See Lifestyle)

Teenie's house, in common with Jim Taylor's and other two-up two-downs, had an outside toilet in the yard. It was of the type known as a dry toilet, a comfortable wooden seat over a large wooden box, situated in a small out-house at the end of the yard, beside the backyard's door that led to an entry behind the house.

Belfast Municipal Corporation sent men around to the empty the toilets approximately every three or four months. They did it one day when I was there. The smell was appalling. It seemed to permeate the bare bones of Auntie Teenie's house along with the rest of the neighbourhood. My cousin, Jim, and I weren't allowed to play in the street that day. I wasn't allowed to observe closely because of the 'germs', so I don't know how many men were involved. They came with a large cart and horse and pushed wheelbarrows up the back entries behind the houses. Auntie Teenie told me residents had to leave their back doors unbarred to enable the men to enter. When it was her turn there was a loud blatter on the door, a man poked his head round and yelled, 'Mrs, I've come to redd out yer privy.'

I was allowed to peep out the back door because I was born nosy (my mother used to call me 'aspidistra face' because I was always in the window). A man came into the yard pushing a wheelbarrow. He went into the privy, took the top off and started digging the contents out with a spade. I retched because the stench was so awful and Auntie Teenie pulled me back indoors. When he'd finished he shouted, 'All done Mrs, ye hadn't as many visitors this time. She was only half full!' and disappeared back into the entry. The full wheelbarrows were taken to the cart and the contents emptied into it.

Comparatively few houses had bathrooms, so it was difficult to keep clean. The vast majority of people washed at the kitchen sink. Saturday night was bath night, when a large zinc bath was dragged out in front of the fire and filled with cold water that was warmed by hot water that had been heated in the kettle on the stove. Filling the bath was an arduous business so the one lot of water was used by the entire family. As a general rule, the youngest child was the first bathed, then sent to bed.

Sewage disposal and water supply in rural areas was just as inadequate as that in Belfast. **Billy W.** was born near Dromore in what he describes as 'a wee cottage in the townland of Ballaney on the Barronstown Road'. The cottage was about 200 yards from a farm, to which it belonged. Like most of the cottages at the time, it had no electric, no gas supply, and no running water.

Billy says, 'The cottage had a water butt that collected water from the roof. There was also a well. Unfortunately if the weather was very cold the well froze over, leaving the family dependent on the water butt. My grandfather, **John Andy Magill**, was born in a house opposite what is now known as Magill's Dam, called after the Magill family.

'I remember him getting up out of bed at five o'clock in the morning, going outside, breaking ice off the top of the water butt and giving himself a good wash. It didn't matter what the weather was like, Granda washed himself in the water butt before going to work. They don't make men like that nowadays!

'Water was stored in buckets in a line along the wall beside the door. It was used for cooking, washing clothes, washing the floors. We had stone floors in the kitchen and pantry while the living room was floored with linoleum. Every Saturday night we had a bath. When we were wee a small zinc bath was pulled out onto the scullery floor and filled with warm water heated in a gas boiler. The scullery was freezing so we used to push towels and newspapers around the windows and doors to keep the draughts out. Boiling water was scarce, because the boiler was small, so we used the same bath water. When we got bigger we washed in an outhouse. My older brother was

the cleanest, so he went first. I was always last to be washed because I played a lot of sport and was usually covered in mud. When I'd finished, the water looked like soup and the bath water was poured into a drain under the water butt, where it ran into another drain and away down the field. Brrrrrr! I'm telling you, you did your level best to get washed, dried and dressed as quickly as possible before running across the yard into the house.

Young Andrew playing on the road. (Printed with kind permission of Billy W.)

'My mother washed the dishes in a container on the table. Water was heated on a two-ring gas stove. We also had a large range on which we kept two or three kettles full of boiling water.

'We had a two-seater, dry toilet in a stone-built shed in the garden. The seat was very comfortable and it was lovely sitting out there in good weather looking at the hen house. The water in the drain washed the effluent away to the bottom of the field. If there'd been a heavy snowfall it wasn't so pleasant as we had to take a shovel and dig a path down to the toilet. We always closed the door in stormy weather. There was trapdoor in the back of the toilet used to clean it out.'

Jay, who lived in Ballinderry, writes, 'Like many other rural homesteads we didn't have the luxury of a mains water supply. Without mains water, we had to obtain our own. Rainwater was kept in tanks and used for most purposes, but drinking water had to be carried from the village pump, and that was the children's job. While our house had a roomy bathroom with a handsome bath and washbasin, it had no toilet, so we did as our predecessors had done and used the two-seater outside dry toilet, though as sophisticated people, we occupied it one at a time. Still, I had a vision of better things. When I accompanied my father to the stock market in Belfast, I insisted on being permitted to pay a private visit to the underground public toilet in Shaftesbury Square, where the tiles glittered, the mahogany doors gleamed and the brass handrail shone like gold and the water flushed perfectly, every time.'

Norah Bates lived in the Down Street, Saintfield, during the Second World War. In her book *Up the Down Street*, describing life in Saintfield, she says her family couldn't afford a hut to house a dry toilet until after the war. Until then they did what they had to do on top of a manure heap.

The situation regarding proper sewage disposal was slow to be rectified. When I worked in what was Ashfield Girl's Secondary School, on the Holywood Road, Belfast, in the 1960s many of the girls lived in houses without proper sanitation. **François Vincent** discovered items recorded in the *Banbridge Chronicle* stating Banbridge Rural District Council was faced with a major issue on 11 February 1952 when rats infested sub-standard houses and had access to wells in Scarva. Two people caught leptospiral jaundice within two months. On 5 June 1961 a trade unionist expressed his disgust that workers assigned to 'bin and pit' duties had to clean out sewage 'with their bare hands'!

Samuel Finlay.

Nobody used toilet paper. Local newspapers were cut, or torn into squares, a hole was cut into one corner of each square and the squares were stuck on a large nail driven into the wall beside the toilet. This was common practice during and after the war.

My grandfather, **Sam Finlay**, who lived in Joanmount Gardens, Belfast, was a cabinetmaker employed by Harland and Wolff shipyard. He was an expert craftsman and had worked on the first-class cabins of the *Titanic*. (He was invited to be part of the guarantee team and travel on *Titanic*'s first voyage to make sure things functioned properly. He was very disappointed to have to turn the invitation down because my grandmother, **Sarah Finlay**, was ill. In retrospect he said granny's illness had saved his life.) Grandpa made a small, French-polished mahogany box designed to fit squares of newspaper and screwed it to the bathroom wall beside the toilet. When I stayed with my grandparents I joined the Saturday night ritual when everyone in the household sat by the fire and cut squares of newspaper to fit the box.

Nigel McKelvey's father owned a business in the centre of Belfast. The family lived in an upmarket house between the Stranmillis and Malone Roads and he remembers the newspaper squares hanging on the nail on the door of his inside toilet. He says, '*The Listener* (a magazine published by the BBC) made better toilet paper than the *Belfast Telegraph* or the *Belfast Newsletter* because the paper was softer.'

Newspaper print made our hands dirty, so we wondered if we ended up with phrases printed on our bottoms. My mother's best friend, who I knew as Auntie Sally, came from County Fermanagh. She went to spend a week with her sister, Annie, and came back saying she had used the *Fermanagh Herald*. It had an entirely different 'feel' to Belfast newspapers and she wondered if she had 'Enniskillen Cattle Market' printed on her behind!

Local historian **Florence Creighton**, who lives in Lisnaskea, says, 'In rural areas many people didn't used newspapers, they used dock leaves growing in the fields.' **Garnet Chambers** says his family didn't have a dry toilet in a hut. They used the hedge and cleaned themselves with a handful of grass, known as a 'wisp'. Practices like these can have unfortunate results because animals may drop ticks on vegetation that can result in a very sore bottom if they become attached and bore into it!

Lifestyle

Thomas Black recounts, 'I was born between Banbridge and Dromore on Barrack Hill. My father married late in life and we'd nothing to live on apart from his pension, £1 a week as far as I can remember. We couldn't afford any luxuries. The only treats my sister, Jean, and I got were two apples and an orange at Christmas.

'My mother was very much younger that my father. She had a hard life. There were no washing machines in those days. Everything was washed by hand and mother didn't even have a washboard or a mangle to wring the clothes out. She scrubbed the clothes with her hands, or a nail brush, then wrung the water out and hung them to dry on the line outside. Clothes dried outside smell better than those dried inside.

'Mother didn't have an iron, just a tin filled with red hot coals from the fire. It had a handle and she wrapped clothes round her hands to hold it. She didn't do much in the way of ironing. She couldn't with a tin. She used Robin starch on the collars to stiffen them and make them look good. Eventually

A traditional fireplace.

she got a gas iron, but it didn't have a thermostat so she spat on its sole and, depending on the rate at which the spit disappeared, she knew if the iron was hot enough to use, or too hot so it would burn the clothes.

'All our cooking was done over an open fire on a crook and crane. Mother was right-handed so the crook was built into the left of the fire. That meant she could use her left hand to push the crane back and forwards to adjust the heat and use her right hand to stir the contents of the round metal pot hung on it. Like all the other housewives in the country, she baked soda bread, wheaten bread and potato bread on a griddle. She put the soda bread and the wheaten bread on a harnen stand (bread stand) in front of the fire to dry. Wee creatures, called crickets, lived around the hearth and used to chirp for us. A singing cricket was a sign of good luck.

'We couldn't afford meat, but sometimes my father brought some sausages or rissoles home and sometimes he bought scrag ends of bacon in Burnett's big grocery shop in Banbridge's Newry Street. Mother kept it on a large willow pattern plate. Scrag ends were cheaper than whole slices. He brought us the occasional herring in the summer and we had goats that gave us milk and hens for eggs.

'Nothing was ever wasted. It was a case of make do and mend. My mother used to knit our sweaters, darn our socks and mend our clothes. She had an old treadle sewing machine she used to make clothes. I still have it and it still works. I mended my trousers on it the other day.'

I can back up what Thomas says about recycling. When given a parcel wrapped in brown paper tied up in string we carefully flattened the paper, folded it up neatly and saved it for reuse. The string was also reused, as was Christmas paper. Even today I have to repress a shudder whenever I see people tearing good paper, screwing it up and throwing it out! Children's clothes were passed down through families or given away. I was always delighted when Auntie Sally brought me dresses that had belonged to her niece Lilian. Food was not wasted, it was recycled. Leftover boiled potatoes were either fried and eaten next day or made into potato bread for breakfast. (All good mothers cooked their children a hearty, cholesterol-filled breakfast before packing them off to school as nobody knew of the harm caused by cholesterol.) We put waste vegetables and such things as potato peelings in a bucket in an outdoor cupboard for the 'pig man'. He arrived once a week carrying two huge buckets that he clattered on the ground beside the cupboard, lifted out our bucket, emptied it into one of his buckets before disappearing out of the garden on up the street to next door. I was always intrigued by his huge feet in their gigantic muddy boots. I have no idea where the 'pig man' came from, what he did when his buckets where full or how he got to our street. All I can say is he appeared to be on foot.

Jim Taylor writes, 'Sam the pig man kept pigs behind the houses in Fourth Street, off Belfast's Shankill Road. He had a few old prams, which we would collect and go around the houses in the area collecting potato peelings, food waste, hard bread, etc. We would get paid a few pence depending on the amount collected. Sam would boil this up in a large metal tank fired by old wood and make pig swill.

'It was a very tough life, but we were happy. We just got on with it. Everyone was in the same boat so we didn't know what we were missing. Young ones today don't know they're living and my father lived until he was eighty!'

If the family was large there weren't enough beds to go round and children slept at the top and the bottom of the bed. When I was lecturing in the Department of Continuing Education at Queen's University Belfast one of my students told me he and his five brothers slept in the same bed and he went to sleep sucking his brother's big toe. Sometimes one of his brothers wet the bed and they'd wake up feeling cold and damp.

Many families didn't have enough blankets, so the bed was piled with overcoats, referred to as 'blankets with pockets', and sheets were a rarity. Some families didn't have proper mattresses and slept on bags filled with straw. Sometimes children were blinded when a piece of straw poked out of the bag and stuck into an eye.

Jay lived on a prosperous farm in Ballinderry. She writes, 'We lived much as people had lived for hundreds of years, with no mains or electricity or water, we used simple tools for most jobs. Our mainstay was our black iron range, on which we did all our cooking. It also heated our living area (the rest of the house was unheated, except when we had visitors or when we three children had measles and were confined to one darkened, fire-lit room for the duration of the illness). Food was simple and traditional: a small roast on Sunday, lots of vegetables, proudly produced by my father, and a monthly delivery of basic rations goods from the firm that held our precious ration books. We had our own potatoes, but unfortunately none of us liked potatoes, and our own eggs and chickens, but we were not keen on eggs, and the chickens had been our friends before they were hung, heads down, in the pantry doorway, and we did not wish to act like cannibals.

Oil lamps (Printed with kind permission of Florence Chambers)
Left to right: Lamp that sat on a table or dresser; Lamp that hung from a hook on the wall; Lamp that could be carried out to inspect the hens.

'The range had to be blackened, the brass candlesticks on the mantelpiece polished, the fourteen lamps washed, their wicks trimmed or replaced. Carpets were swept by a rotary cleaner, or in the case of stairs and under beds, by hand brush. There was a solid iron knocker on the front door, while the back door, to which most callers came, was always unlocked and so did not need a knocker. We, like most people, did not have a telephone, but my grandfather had a handsome two-part phone set which could be used in emergencies. There were, of course no televisions, or mobile phones and so, I suppose, life was much quieter than it is today. We had a piano, lots of books and lively imaginations when it came to exploring outdoors.

'We lived within a small area, as most of us travelled on foot or by bicycle, as cars spent the war shut in the garage. Most of our needs were met by local people who lived in or near the village. The shoe mender was still a practising shoemaker and displayed handmade wooden lasts carefully carved to the foot size and shape of each of his customers. He worked from home, as did the dressmaker and the barber. The schoolteachers lived in accommodation provided near each school. The clergymen lived locally and the doctor's surgery was attached to his house, and provided a waiting room of notable austerity of damp, coughing people patiently waiting their turn. Doctors provided home visits when necessary, and most babies were delivered at home, with the local midwife also in attendance. Illnesses such as measles, mumps, chickenpox and tuberculosis were commonplace – I got them all!

'My grandmother's coffin was borne with great dignity in a black carriage drawn by black horses. We watched its departure from the door of our house, as women and children did not at that time follow the hearse to the graveyard. Tuberculosis attacked some families especially cruelly. Special huts appeared in gardens, as far as possible from the house, to accommodate the current invalid and try to prevent the disease from attacking other members of the family. I acquired bovine tuberculosis from the butter we obtained from a nearby farm where the cattle had the disease. Health and safety were not as closely monitored as they are now.

'During the '30s, '40s and '50s children in urban areas, like country children, wandered around at will. The only time parents ever saw us was at mealtimes and nobody worried.'

I myself was 3 years of age when, during the Second World War, I was taken by my mother, **Anne Henry** (née Finlay), to visit her aunts **Bella, Lizzie and Aggie Finlay**. They lived at Skilginaban near Ballynure and I had the opportunity of seeing an entirely different lifestyle to the one I was used to in Belfast.

Bella, Aggie and Lizzie were typical kindly country folk. They made us very welcome and said they were making her favourite Irish stew for lunch.

Mum said she couldn't wait to get 'stuck into it'. She remembered enjoying it as a child when she'd spent her school holidays with them. In the past the air in Belfast was very polluted so Granda Finlay's siblings looked after his children during school holidays to give them some healthy, clean country fresh air.

Mum used to tell me stories about working in the fields, following their five cows to the byre at milking time, the beautiful smell of meadowsweet and honeysuckle, the garden she used to play in. She was bathed on Saturday nights in a large tin bath in front of the fire, then taken upstairs and tucked up in a cosy bed covered by patchwork quilts made out of old tweed coats. She said the smell of lavender on linen sheets always reminded her of her aunts. I found the most impressive story of all was about the companionship found when using the seven-seater toilet in the byre. Mum said, 'About five o'clock somebody would say, "Does anyone feel like going to clock?"' and a group would go into the byre, occupy the seats, and have 'lovely wee conversations' while doing their business. In those far-off days proper sewage facilities were rare.

My great grandfather, **Arthur Hill Finlay**, never used the seven-seater. He like me, demanded privacy, so he had his own private spot among the rhododendron bushes in the garden. The rhododendrons were never the same after he died. I had the opportunity of using the seven-seater during my visit, but I, like great grandfather Finlay, demanded privacy! I firmly refused, although I was told that by the time I got home I'd be 'Bustin' my boiler!' I was! But I managed to reach home without having an accident!

The sisters cooked using an old-fashioned crook and crane with a black iron pot suspended from it. Delicious smells wafted round the room and their soda bread and scones were so light they melted in the mouth.

I liked the kitchen. It was comfortable and homely, but I didn't like what happened next! A 'thing' walked out of the bottom of the wall.

Aunt Lizzie said, 'Oh! The wee dear! Wait until you see this Doreen!' She dusted some flour on the hearth and a whole lot of the 'things' came out from under the wall and started making funny noises. Aunt Liz said, 'Crickets, they bring luck. The wee dears! Aren't they lovely.'

I was not impressed. I felt they were dirty, like house flies, and wondered if it was safe to eat that stew, but it smelt delicious so I followed my mother's example and took the advice to 'get tore in'.

An elderly man, **Andy McMinn**, came in. He was wearing an old duncher and smoking a pipe. He was made very welcome and settled down in a grandfather chair at the side of the fire with a cup of tea and one of those delicious scones. He said he'd just come in for the craic and the aunts and my mother said, 'Go'n Andy, gie us a song!'

At first Andy refused, then my mother said, 'I'd love to hear an "Auld Cum All Ye". I haven't heard one for years.'

Andy smiled and began, 'Cum all ye fine people, and listen til my song, It's only forty verses and t'will not keep ye long,' and intoned verses that had everyone, except me, in kinks of laughter. I couldn't understand a word!

On the way home in the bus I asked Mum why I couldn't understand and she said that was because they were using the 'old language'. I asked why everyone was laughing. She said the song was 'rude'. She was reluctant to tell me, but eventually did. It was about a local Presbyterian church hall that had dances on Saturday nights. Like most halls, it didn't have what we would regard as proper toilet facilities. There was a room upstairs to which the girls retired at the interval for a comfort break. It had a row of 'potties' along one wall for their use. The boys who set up the room, decided to play a joke and placed some baking soda in each of the potties and when the girls did their business they got a shock when froth came up round their bottoms. Big Lizzie was so upset she fainted and had to be carried home!

Years later I had the privilege of getting to know local historian the late **Ernie Scott** and his wife **Marjorie**. I questioned Ernie about my memory. He laughed and said, 'Fancy you remembering that! The man concerned was **Andy McMinn**. He was great at singing "Cum All Yees". The church hall was Straid Presbyterian Church and I'm ashamed to say I was one of the big ligs who put the baking soda in the goes-unders (potties, goes under the bed, hence the name, goes-under)! I felt awful afterwards. Poor Lizzie. I shouldn't

Ernest Scott.

have done that! She never married. She had a face you'd not like to waken up next to and a smile like the handle on a coffin! She didn't need me to play jokes on her.'

I still have a very soft spot in my heart for the area around Ballynure and the happy memories of all those people who are long gone.

Education

In the North the Catholic Church was allowed to set up its own school system, separate from the state system, which was meant to educate all catholic children. (Protestants were, wisely, not allowed to set up a separate system in the South. A divided school system leads to a divided society.) Today the vast majority of the population recognise that great wrongs occurred on both sides of the fence and are determined that things will be different in the future. There is a growing movement for integrated education, where Catholic and Protestant children are educated together. The ethos of an integrated school is not to change anyone's religion but to give a deep, tolerant understanding of differing beliefs.

Before, during and until shortly after the war, comparatively wealthy parents paid for their children to have a secondary education in what was called a grammar school, such as Portadown College, the Methodist College Belfast (Methody), Lurgan College, Coleraine Academical Institution, Rainey Endowed, Enniskillen Royal and Campbell College, which had boarding departments. Very wealthy parents often sent their children as boarders to public schools such as Roedean, Rugby, Eton, Harrow, Winchester and so on in England. Only 12 per cent of people went to university.

In effect, unless your parents were wealthy you had very little chance of getting a secondary education. You might win a scholarship but scholarships were few and far between. Things changed in 1947 with the Education Act passed by the Westminster government in England during 1944 and the introduction of what was called the 'Qualifying Examination'. We're always behind England so it didn't come into force in Northern Ireland until 1947. It said everybody had to have a secondary education. You had to go to another school when you were 11. You had to sit written exams that included verbal reasoning and numeracy tests. If you passed that you could go to a grammar school, otherwise you went to what was called a 'secondary intermediate school'. That was when the names of schools changed and public elementary schools became primary schools.

George McBride recalls, 'My first school was the free public elementary school in Longstone Street, Lisburn (See Chapter 6). With 1945 came the end of the war and not long afterwards we returned to our old home, 17 Bloomfield Street, in East Belfast. I was immediately enrolled in my second school, East Bread Street Public Elementary School, where not only did I continue with the 3Rs but was also introduced by two inspirational teachers, **Jimmy Stephenson** and headmaster **John Lowry**, to English Literature via the novels of Robert Louis Stevenson and even William Shakespeare, to be specific, *Julius Caesar*! In our weekly visits to Templemore Avenue swimming baths, I also learned to swim. Lowry told me about a new examination and that he was going to enter my name to "take it". As it turned out, this was the Northern Ireland 1947 Education Act, designed to introduce free secondary education for all children in the province. It was the first "Qualifying Examination" in Northern Ireland and I "qualified", so was able to have a secondary education, something that had been denied to my elder brother, John. In September 1948 I was enrolled in my third school, the grammar school then known as Grosvenor High School, in West Belfast.

Several of the teaching staff were ex-service personnel and that was where I first met **Miss Grosse**, a German national.' (See Chapter 7 Prisoners of War.)

Margaret Graham was reared in Banbridge and spent the first three years of her schooling in the Church Street School, Banbridge, which was situated where Holy Trinity's Church Hall is now. She says, 'Schools were very different from schools today. Church Street, like many others at the time had no internal walls. Some schools had all the classes in one large schoolroom. The Church Street School was divided into three classrooms by curtains. It was possible to hear what was going on in other classes.'

George Wilson attended a rural school and records, 'I was raring to go to school but I caught ringworm from handling my father's calves and wasn't allowed to do so until May 1945. In those days, without modern medication, ringworm was hard to control. It started off as a rough red patch on my hand, spread to my legs and then I got it all over my back. I wasn't allowed to touch it. I was taken to the doctor in Gilford and he kept treating me with salves. They didn't work so eventually he got me to take my shirt off and lie on a couch under a sun ray lamp. That worked. In August 1946 I caught scarlet fever and spent four weeks in Lurgan Hospital. I wasn't allowed out for two weeks after I was discharged. Scarlet fever was a terrifying disease that was very infectious and it was a killer.

George Wilson's school. (Printed with kind permission of George Wilson —the tallest boy in the back row)

'I was 6 years of age when I started Ballydougan Public Elementary School, a wee country school about half a mile from Bleary, and I really enjoyed it. When I started there were about ninety pupils. On my first day I joined six or seven other children walking across the fields to school. Other children joined us on the way. It was a mixed school with about sixty Protestants and thirty Roman Catholics. I think that's the way schools should be. I loved Ballydougan Primary School and still treasure the photo of all the pupils taken in 1951 during my last year there. I'm the tallest boy in the back row, although the boys beside me were older. I think I grew big and strong because of all the dung on my boots!

'I've been told the number of pupils went up to more than 120 during the Blitz. Bombs falling on Belfast had people fearing for their lives, so they left the city and came into the country as refugees. Their children attended local schools. Country schools became overcrowded and city ones emptied. Children who had been in the Blitz were jumpy and couldn't concentrate. There were only two teachers for the whole school, so that must have been very difficult – 120 pupils, two teachers and no classroom assistants!

'There were about forty pupils when I left Ballydougan Public Elementary School. Then a lot more houses were built in Bleary and Gilford and people moved to housing estates. The local priest came and sounded the death knell of my wee school. He came to the school on a Friday and said to the Roman Catholic pupils, "You have to go to a new school, St John's Primary School in Gilford on Monday." The numbers of the old school fell after that, it was closed and the remaining pupils were transferred to Bleary Primary School.

'Classes had different names in those days from what they have today. We had baby infants, senior infants, then first class, second class, and so on up to Class 6. Everybody went to the public elementary school until they reached school leaving age at 14. When I started school in Ballydougan the first three classes were taken by the one teacher. Imagine that! The equivalent of our P1, P2 and P3 all in one class! Teachers could use a cane to knock some sense into children who were misbehaving and that helped with discipline. Many's the hard slap I got on my hand, two or three at a time! It didn't do me any harm.

'I loved Ballydougan school. We played football, Rangers versus Celtic, and a great game of chasing the girls into the laurel bushes, or behind the bicycle sheds. Men around our part of the country said you got a good all-round education at Ballydougan!

'A lot of the children, especially the girls, went just down the road into Blanes Handkerchief Factory, when they were 14. The girls either embroidered handkerchiefs, or became seamstresses and the boys learnt how to service and look after the machines. Some pupils found leaving school upsetting because they loved learning, were very good at school work and would have liked to continue with their education but I suppose their parents needed the money they brought in.

'At primary school we did reading, writing and arithmetic. We could count and we knew our multiplication tables off by heart. We didn't need fancy calculators. We did calculations in our heads and we did algebra. I loved writing. We had work books called Vere Foster Copy books. They had lines of good writing and you had to copy it on the empty lines below. I liked that and in 1951, the year of the Festival of Britain, I won a certificate for good handwriting in a national handwriting competition organised by *The Children's Newspaper*. In the springtime we grew vegetables, such as peas and beans, for half an hour each week. There was no clock in the field so we used to put our spades away early and be home at 2.30!

'I left Ballydougan Primary School when I was 14 and went to Lurgan Technical College. I hated it. We had to do about ten subjects and I just couldn't cope. I was like a wild hare in a chase. I was too fond of being out in the fields working with my father and local farmers, tractor driving, ploughing and sowing corn to settle in the tech.

I myself was educated in Belfast, so had a very different experience to George Wilson, although the names of classes were similar. My first school was the preparatory department of Bloomfield Collegiate on the Newtownards Road. I hated it. The school has changed tremendously since then. It's on a different site and no longer has a preparatory department.

In retrospect my class, 'the babies' class, had a bad teacher. She was covered in gentle smiles and sat in the corner. I don't remember her ever standing up. She had no idea, or didn't care, about what was going on in her class. We were left to play together. One small sturdy boy was addicted to playing with a doll's pram. He spent the day pretending it was a car and running me over. It hurt. I screamed and teacher never noticed. To be fair, I wasn't the only one he attempted to kill. I had periods of relief during which he ran over other pupils, but I was definitely his favourite so I spent most of the day crying.

Every now and then teacher used to call somebody up to hear their reading. At home my parents were avid readers and I was surrounded by books. Mum told me the marks inside a book were like magic. They told you about far away people and places and through them you could escape to another world. We had a book that started with, 'The cat sat on the mat'. It was the opposite of exciting and I don't remember getting as far as the second page. I just didn't 'get' learning to read through 'look and say'. I felt stupid and I hated being continually thumped with a doll's pram so every day I screamed all the way to school. Eventually somebody suggested it might be a good idea if I changed school, so I started Harding Memorial on Belfast's Cregagh Road and loved it.

Harding Memorial was a large school that took pride in being up to date, so it had what were called 'mixed classes', in other words boys and girls were taught together. It didn't have 'babies'. It had 'infants' and I was a senior mixed infant in a class of sixty! It was towards the end of the war, refugee children had returned to the city and there was a shortage of teachers because so many had joined the armed forces, or were helping with the war effort.

Mrs Armstrong was our teacher and she was wonderful. We sat in twos on old-fashioned desks and behaved ourselves. Frankly I don't know how she managed. She didn't even have a classroom assistant. She had a cane but rarely used it and if forced to do so appeared very upset. She taught reading through phonetics. I 'got' that and very quickly learned to read. We learned to write using a piece of chalk on a slate board and were very excited when we changed to pen and ink. You had to be very careful because a dip pen and ink could make an awful mess. As well as reading, writing and arithmetic we learnt to sew, did art and had our paintings displayed on noticeboards near us. That was a great incentive. We made sculptures from plasticine, building them on wooden boards. We enjoyed singing and PE. If you went into a school there was always some class having a singing lesson. I blossomed. Mrs Armstrong encouraged pupils to do their best.

Orangefield Primary School opened its doors in 1946 [it celebrated its seventy-fifth anniversary on 4 June 2021] and my parents decided to send me there. It was fine except for **Miss Kennedy**, my Class 6 teacher [the equivalent of our P7]. She was a sadist! The boys in my class were of one opinion. No man in his right mind would marry Miss Kennedy. She was small and skinny with a forbidding expression, blood red lips, hard coal eyes and a pale blotchy complexion. She shouted abuse and wielded the cane with enthusiasm. She terrorised us. If you got less than seven out of ten for any piece of work you received a slap, with a cane, on your hand, for each mistake. Each day we were given a small bottle of sour milk to drink. The first time that happened I explained milk made me sick, so I got a slap and was told to drink it before she returned, or else (I'm lactose intolerant). Luckily one of the boys saw my predicament. He gave me his empty bottle, drank my milk for me and continued to do so throughout the year.

I remember also the linen knickers I was given to sew. They were cut on the large side to allow for growth and were a work of art, with run and fell seams and hem stitching. I never grew big enough to fill them.

At that time Orangefield Primary School didn't have indoor toilets. It had a toilet block in the playground. Each day Miss Kennedy marched us out during our break and insisted we line up and use them.

I rebelled! I decided I was not going to expose my nether regions to the cold, frosty air. I wisely kept quiet about my intentions, entered the cubicle, stood in from of the toilet facing the door for several minutes, pulled the chain and came out. She never caught on! I was taking a big risk because Miss Kennedy used to look under the door to see if your feet were in the right place and sometimes, if she suspected rebellion, would tell you not to pull the chain until she inspected what had been produced.

Bad as that was, it was nothing to what went on in the old Donacloney Primary School. When I went to teach in Dromore High School during the 1980s my pupils told me it had dry toilets suspended over the River Lagan. There was a fastidious caretaker who used to don wellingtons, walk along the river bed and whitewash the inside of the toilets, and if you were sitting on them at the time you got your behind whitewashed, too!'

Shopping

The first supermarket in Northern Ireland, Supermac, opened in 1964 at what is now Forestside. It changed shopping beyond belief. Until that time you either bought goods off hawkers who travelled from door to door or you went to a local shop. There was no such thing as a one-stop shop.

Jim Taylor writes, 'We had Sammy, who came around weekly with a handcart with basins full of fish, mainly herring. He called out, "Herns Come to the cart and see them winking."

'We had regular traders like the bread server from Inglis bakery, called William. He would pull out massive drawers containing all sorts of bakery products, the housewives picked what they wanted and took them away, unwrapped. Hygiene was in its infancy.

'Fred the knife sharpener was used by people who didn't use their jawbox [sink] to sharpen their knives. He came on a bike and put it on a stand, sat on the handlebars and peddled backwards turning the grindstone, which was driven by the back wheel. As most families had a few knives, Fred did good business.

'We had a special visitor one summer. It was a French onion seller complete with beret and bike with string of onions hanging from the handlebars. We thought he had a funny accent.

'The lemonade man from Cantrell and Cochrane sold large bottles of lemonade from the back of his lorry. We could take the empty bottles back to the shop at the corner of Fifth Street and get a few pence back. The bottles were stored in the yard behind the shop in crates. The wall was about 5ft high, so at night we would climb over and take a few bottles to claim the money back. The shopkeeper got wise to this and put a pencil mark on the edge of the labels. If you returned one of these you got a thick ear. I can still feel the pain!'

I have similar memories to Jim. We had deliveries of bread, milk, vegetables and lemonade. Housewives went out to delivery vans and chose what they wanted. My mother bought from the Ormo Bakery bread van, which was a regal purple colour and powered by an electric motor! It was a slow, stately affair. The milkman was my favourite tradesman. He had a horse and cart. The horse was a huge Clydesdale, a powerful, friendly animal called Hamlet. I used to feed it hunks of bread. During school holidays Hamlet clattered up the street, without the milkman, and stopped outside my door, where he soulfully chewed the privet hedge until I appeared and gave him his treat. Hamlet had another bonus. He left droppings around the neighbourhood and I used to race to sweep them up to feed my roses.

My cat Panda's favourite tradesman was the fisherman! He walked around the neighbourhood shouting something that sounded like, 'Heeeeriiiin ali-iiiiiiiiive!' Panda yowled with pleasure when he heard the cry and yelled with pleasure as he rushed to greet the fisherman, who gave him herring heads. You had a choice of fish, big herrings, or wee herrings! Other types of fish were unknown.

Travelling salesman's bread van. (Printed with kind permission of Florence Chambers)

Florence Chambers says, 'During the war my mother bought goods from travelling salesmen. We were very dependent on them because it was a long walk from our house into Dromore. After the war, when a limited amount of petrol became available for private use [petrol rationing didn't end until 1950] my mother took the car, parked it and we walked, carrying a basket, round to a shop, formed an orderly queue beside the counter and waited to be served by a shop assistant.

'Grocers' shops had goods, such as biscuits, held in large hessian bags that were lined with paper, sitting in front of the counter. There were tea chests full of tea. Legs of bacon sat on the counter and individual slices were carved off for individual customers. I was always interested in the resident cat that sat beside a leg of cooked ham on the counter. We thought the ham was delicious and so did the resident cat. It used to sit and lick the ham! Over-packaging was unknown as plastic did not exist. Nothing was boxed, apart from chocolates. Sweets were displayed in large bottles and goods were placed in brown paper bags and put into your shopping basket to be carried home.

'Some real foods were in very short supply, or unavailable, so housewives made the best they could of such things as dried eggs and banana essence. Real coffee was a rarity but there were tall slim bottles of Camp coffee, which was a liquid made from chicory and it was very sweet.'

Pet shop, Garfield Street, Smithfield.

As a child I found being sent for a message to my local grocery, which was at the corner of Trigo Parade on the Castlereagh Road, a nightmare. Children were taught to be 'seen and not heard', to give their seats to adults and to allow adults to go in front of them in a queue. Once I stood for over an hour. My mother became very worried as she thought I'd had an accident or something. She rushed round to the shop and quickly ascertained what was happening. I was standing meekly beside the counter and I was fed up. I wanted to go out to play and was close to tears. Another woman came in and the assistant began to serve her. Mum was usually mild mannered but she saw red and practically shouted, 'That child must have been standing there for over an hour. Good manners are one thing, but fair's fair. You should have made sure she was served in a reasonable amount of time!' I never had to wait so long again!

I loved to visit a pet shop in Smithfield. I could have stood for hours watching goldfish, mice, puppies and kittens on display.

The Importance of Radio and the News

'We listened to what we called the wireless', **Jay** writes. 'We relied very much on the radio to keep us informed. Before six o'clock every evening my father sat close to the wireless set to hear the news. [My father did the same. Indeed I believe every family in the province listened to the six o'clock news if they possibly could.] We knew not to disturb the daily ritual. The programmes featured English voices, speaking what was known as BBC English. Programmes in Ulster idiom didn't exist until 1948, when the BBC commissioned Joseph Tomelty to write a weekly saga of working-class life in Belfast and *The McCooeys* were born. For the first time outside the field of documentary, ordinary Ulster people could hear their own voices. The series lasted for seven years and life in Ulster stopped every Saturday night while locals listened to the still relatively new medium of radio. If you walked along any street during the time *The McCooeys* were being broadcast you could have heard the complete episode through open doors and windows. During the following week what had happened during the programme was the main topic of conversation.'

Street Games

BMJ, who lived in Strabane during the war, remembers playing with friends. He says, 'Children on our street had a great time playing after school and in the holidays. Because of the war there was no petrol except for certain urgent cases. So we played in the middle of the road! We marked out hopscotch on the middle of Strabane's Main Street. We also got a long skipping rope and two people were appointed to wind it while the rest queued up to take turns, skipping in and out. We played marbles in the gutter, boys and girls – there would be up to twenty children taking part. We formed a big circle on the road for the singing games. If a horse and cart came along we just all stood back till it passed.'

My own war memories in Belfast are similar to BMJ's. I played in the street. My mother used to tie a rope to the top of a lamp post and we took it in turns to swing round it. I loved swinging around a lamp post at dusk. It was magical. Girls played skipping games while boys played cowboys and Indians, or raced gliders (small carts, built with some sort of wheel, such as ball bearings or pram wheels with an axle that allowed them to be steered) down hills at breakneck speed. There was always great rivalry about who had the fastest glider and frequent fisticuffs! Sometimes we played pole vaulting in the middle of the road, using long garden canes.

A favourite pastime was to remove the heavy metal drain covers and use sticks to poke down them to see if anyone had dropped a valuable in there. Unfortunately we never found anything, although several of the boys lost their fingertips while replacing the cover! Today our actions would cause health and safety to have a hairy fit but in the past nobody worried about what we were doing. I still remember the slight smell of sewage rising from the drain and in retrospect wonder why we didn't catch some ghastly disease! We were expected to be responsible for ourselves so if we hurt ourselves we were more likely to get a good hiding for being stupid rather than sympathy!

Once in the middle of a game we heard a car had driven into Manna Grove! Somebody said it was a limousine! A car was a rare sight, never mind a limousine! Nobody had ever seen one before. Our game was immediately ditched and we rushed into Manna Grove.

It was a funeral! We'd never seen a funeral before and we thought it was great! There were three limousines and a strange car we learned was a hearse. (We were about 5 years of age at the time and didn't understand what had happened.) We were mesmerised as a coffin was carried out of the house. People stood around outside looking very serious. The coffin was placed in the hearse and covered with flowers. The hearse drove slowly up the street followed by three limousines filled with women, a couple of cars and approximately 100 men wearing dark suits and carrying proper hats, not just the usual dunchers (flat caps). We were goggle-eyed and decided to play funerals.

There was a small rough patch of soil behind my garage. It was supposed to be a vegetable garden, part of the 'dig for victory' campaign, but it flooded and never grew anything more interesting than slugs. We decided that would make a suitable grave. Jane went home and reappeared with a shoebox to use as a coffin. We put an old doll with no arms in it, made wreaths of daisy and dandelion flowers, used a wheelbarrow as the hearse, put on our most solemn faces and paraded around the street before digging a hole in the 'graveyard' and burying the doll. Freda said her daddy came home from a funeral and said, 'Ashes to ashes, dust to dust, if the drink don't get ye, the women must.' Somehow that seemed appropriate so we pretended to cry as we chanted it over the 'grave'!

Going to the Pictures (Movies)

George Nesbitt says, 'When I was a teenager I loved going to Banbridge Picture House to see what we called "the pictures". The old picture house, like all picture houses at the time, had only one auditorium with one screen. Entrance was 6*d*, that's six pennies in old money, until the price doubled to one shilling (12*d*)! My friends and I were raging and staged a protest by not going for about six weeks. Our strike had absolutely no effect on the management, we missed our weekly shot of the pictures, gave in and started attending again.

'Going to the pictures was very different from attending the movies today. There were no sweets, no ice cream and no popcorn. There tended to be a lot of noise as we cheered cowboys and Indians. I don't know why I never saw any of Charlie Chaplin's movies. I know his wartime masterpiece, *The Great Dictator*, was shown to enthusiastic audiences at the Banbridge Picture House on 10 February 1941. I'm sorry I missed it. I'm sure I'd have enjoyed his antics. Early Charlie Chaplin movies were silent and children used to wonder how he could be made to talk.

'The projector in the Picture House often broke down. We stamped our feet and made a whale of a noise until the show was resumed! It was fun!

'I walked to the Picture House from our family farm in Seapatrick because there weren't any buses at night time. Life became easier when I got a bicycle for my 14th birthday. After that I cycled into town and parked it, along with the other bicycles, up Beck's entry beside Beck's Garage in Newry Street, where the Windsor Bakery is now. I was terribly upset one night when I went to collect my bicycle and it had disappeared. I was in despair as I walked home. Thankfully it had only been borrowed so it turned up again.

'My parents never knew I went to the pictures. I kept it on the QT because they were strict Presbyterians and would not have approved. My grandfather had been Clerk of Sessions in Castlewellan Presbyterian Church, by father was an elder in Bannside Presbyterian Church. I was also an elder and my son has followed in my footsteps. He's now an elder in Bannside Presbyterian Church.

'I did another unusual thing for a Presbyterian. I learned to dance in the Temperance Hall. It didn't hold dancing classes, but I always managed to get a partner who taught me the steps.'

When I was growing up Belfast had forty cinemas. The less salubrious ones were known as 'flea pits'. There were Saturday morning clubs for children. I didn't have sufficient pocket money to be able to go very often but sometimes I went with my friends to a local picture house (cinema). Children living in my part of the Castlereagh Road usually went to The Ambassador on the Cregagh Road. It was near Harding Memorial Public Elementary School. (It now houses Wyse Byes.) We screamed our heads off with excitement at 'cowboy and Indian' movies. We didn't say we were 'going to a cinema to see a movie' we went to a 'picture house to see a film'. It's strange how language changes over time! Picture houses were very different from cinemas today as there was only one screen.

I have to admit the excitement I felt watching the antics of Hopalong Cassidy and Roy Rogers with his horse, Trigger, surpasses anything I've ever felt ever since. The cowboys' mission was to fight the 'Red Indians', earn the love of a good woman, then leave her and ride off into the sunset. Years later, I attended a lecture given by the late Seamus Heaney and he said, 'A child is a very complicated thing. It has all the emotions of an adult. What it lacks is a framework in which to hang them.' Those old cowboy movies aroused all sorts of emotions, and yearnings! In retrospect I'm appalled by their implicit racist and sexist messages. 'Red Indians' were always the bad guys, while the white cowboys were 'good'.

Strand Cinema. (Printed with kind permission of the now Strand Arts Centre)

Antique 25mm projector originally used in the Strand. (Printed with kind permission of Strand Arts Centre)

There was a picture house further down the Castlereagh Road from where I lived, called the Castle. We weren't allowed to go there because our parents said it was 'too rough'! On rare occasions we walked to the Strand Picture House on the Holywood Road. It's the only surviving cinema in Northern Ireland from the golden age of movies. It's a lovely art nouveau building, still showing movies and used as a community arts centre.

I loved visiting **Auntie Teenie** (see previous), who lived in 9 Morpeth Street, off the Shankill Road, especially when she'd saved enough empty jam jars to allow me, cousin Jim and some of his friends into the Shankill Picturedrome, on the corner of Northumberland Street and Shankill Road. We beamed from ear to ear as we carried our jam jars round to the picture house and presented them to Joe in the ticket kiosk. We felt very important because instead of exchanging our jam jars for a ticket to the stalls, he winked at us and shouted, 'Here's Teenie's kids! They're for the balcony!' We were delighted as we rushed up the stairs to sit in the best seats, for a jam jar! The Shankill Picturedrome was known locally as 'Wee Jo's'. It had a dimly lit bar on the balcony, surrounded by men wearing dunchers (flat caps) in the left-hand corner furthest away from the door.

Auntie Teenie used to line us up before we went and make us promise to stay away from 'the dirty old men' drinking at the bar, and she'd tell my cousin, Jim, to look after me. I thought that was peculiar because I was older than Jim and felt I should look after him! Jim proved his worth as a minder when one of the 'dirty old men' left the bar, came up the stairs in the darkened theatre and began to talk to me. I was embarrassed. I didn't know what to do. I'd been taught to be polite and answer when spoken to. I felt I should say something, but Auntie Teenie had stressed we kept away from the 'dirty old men'. I felt myself blush. Cousin Jim proved equal to the occasion.

He shouted, 'Piss off Mister or I'll tell the attendant!' The man must have broken the Olympic Record for rushing downstairs back to the bar.

Jim's younger brother, **Alan Lyle**, says there was a side door that opened onto Northumberland Street. It was possible to nip in there without paying. The trouble was the open door shone light into the darkened cinema. You were momentarily blinded because you came from bright lights into the dark and you had to find a seat quickly before you got caught, so you raced up the stairs and sat down without knowing if the seat you'd chosen had somebody sitting in it or not!

'Wee Joe's' had a sad end. When Joe retired he sold the cinema. Its character changed and it eventually closed in 1958. The building was destroyed during the Troubles. My cousin, Alan, became Deputy Head of Belfast Fire Brigade and felt it was ironic to be at the site of the old cinema, where he had such happy memories, clearing up after a terrorist bomb.

Freddy Elliot, who lives in Strabane, says he paid 2 pennies to get into his local cinema, the Palindrome, in Strabane. That was comparatively posh, but not nearly as posh as the Picture House in Banbridge, where **George Nesbitt** says he paid a 6d entrance fee until the price was raised to one shilling!

Every town and many villages had at least one picture house: Bangor had two – the Tonic and the Savoy.

Gilford had a picture house (cinema), the Dunbarton, which is now in the Ulster Folk and Transport Museum. On 26 October 1962 its directors arranged a meeting to decide if the old cinema should reopen. It had been closed during the summer months because television had caused a fall in attendance. During its heyday there were full houses practically every night and three changes of programme each week. In 1962 it was only open for three nights a week, attendances were poor and staying open was uneconomical.

Eltico Mills of Gilford opened Gilford Picture House during 1943 to entertain its employees. The girls, and a supervisor, acted as usherettes six nights a week after their normal work.

The Library Service

Evelyn Hanna, who works in the Library Service, writes, 'Modern Ireland has developed from its reputation as "the land of saints and scholars" and that is very true of the North. As a nation we care about education.

'Andrew Carnegie said, "A library outranks any other one thing a community can do to benefit its people. It is a never failing spring in the desert."

'Banbridge library is a typical example of the work of all others throughout the North. It has been at the heart of much that has gone on in the town. It and other libraries, in the difficult years leading up to and during the Second World War, adapted to the changing circumstances around it.

'At that stage the library was in the beautiful red-bricked Carnegie building situated between the Unitarian and Methodist church and close to the railway station. It was therefore in a prime position and central to the town.

'Mr McConkey was appointed joint librarian/caretaker when the library opened in 1902. He was a real character, with a mind of his own. The Library Service would have liked to "lose" him, but couldn't because he was also the building's caretaker! Under Mr McConkey's librarianship you could choose your own books, but that didn't mean you could borrow them! Oh no! Mr McConkey would inspect them, decide whether he thought they were

Building provided for a Carnegie library, Banbridge.

suitable for you and if not he would substitute his choice of books that you could take home.

'In 1939 big changes occurred in Banbridge Library. Mr McConkey retired and a new librarian was appointed. There were also significant changes within the community it served. In October 1939 it was noted that, "the officers and members of the Rifle Brigade be granted permission to become borrowers for the usual terms of sixpence while stationed in the town". A certificate of guarantee had been obtained from the PRI Major Norcete (it was later agreed that they could use the library for free with the brigade making a donation to library funds instead) and by 1940 over 162 of HM Forces had joined and were using the library services.

'The library began to physically adapt to the changing world as air raid procedures were put in place and blackout arrangements were made, with screens being erected to ensure no lights were visible, and the library threw itself with enthusiasm into the war effort, donating £50 during war weapons week. However, where the library was really involved in the local war effort was with the planning and implementing of a book drive.

'The ministry had suggested in 1943 that there could be a province-wide book drive to restock blitzed libraries and provide reading materials for the troops.

'In Banbridge a book drive sub-committee was formed mainly from those on the library committee and arrangements were put in place. It was agreed prizes would be made to the three boys and three girls who collected the most books and a poster competition was also organised. The local schools were all provided with the drawing sheets for the children, who were advised to create slogans on their posters like "I've been on this shelf long enough – now I am going to join up!" and "keep your Bible and your bank book – give all the rest".

'At this meeting it was expressed that in order to make the proposed book drive a success it would be desirable to have the co-operation of all the organisations within the town. The library was naturally the best place for knowing how to contact people and who these organisations were.

'Further plans were put in place and on Monday, 20 September 1943 a loudspeaker van went around the town and after the formal opening, each child was then given a token with the weight of the books they had collected and handed in recorded on it. The week was launched by Miss Douglas of the library committee, who announced, "This is the BBC –

which stands for Banbridge's Book Committee – and here is the news ..."
She told the children:

Clean the shelves of all your books
Look in crannies and in nooks,
Bring them to the centre shop
They will make the German's hop.

'She also advised they get as much publicity as possible:

Write it on the Banbridge walls
Write it on the schoolboys' slate
One more book for Hitler's fate.

'By the fourth day of the book drive, 5 tons of books had been collected.
Some old and valuable books were also found, one dating back to 1638.

'By the end of the fifth day, 9 tons had been gathered in and thank you
notices were put in the local papers. The winning posters and the work of
the young people were all put on display in the book depot, which was in
Newry Street, and Miss Douglas presented the prizes for the best posters to
the children in their various schools and the local *Banbridge Chronicle* carried
the story and the names of all the prize winners.

'The book drive was hailed a great success and the sum of £ 50 5s 2d was
received from the books that were salvaged. Praise was received from many
organisations for the excellent work and careful organisation that the library
committee and staff had carried out.

'In 1944 the report of the Library Association stated that there was a need for
wider consideration of the post-war library service. Banbridge library committee noted these comments and showed their own forward thinking. They
recorded that "in the future the most important institution in every town will
be the library" and "there would have to be more adequate accommodation,
good reference books and the librarian would have great responsibility".

'Keen to build on their success, a second book drive was then organised
for the week 21–28 October 1944. This time all the books were to be taken
to a depot in Commercial Road. All the children collecting books received
a special private's badge. The more books they collected, the higher up the
ranks they climbed:

25 books = sergeant
50 books = captain
150 books = general
250 = field marshal

'A staggering 17,000 books were collected, far exceeding their target of 10,000. Fourteen children reached field marshal status and prizes were awarded. Many of them remained lifelong borrowers and supporters of the library. One such person was Dennis McAleenan, who in later life was to become an avid collector of first edition books, perhaps inspired by his time collecting for this books drive in 1944!

'By 1945 and the end of the war, the library membership exceeded 500, and plans were starting to be made to catalogue all the books in the library. Then, as now, as life began to get back to a new normality the library remained at the heart of the community, a place it still holds today.'

My mother occasionally took me to the library on the Cregagh Road. The books were in very short supply and the librarians were lovely, very helpful and very apologetic for the lack of books. I remember discussing Ladybird books with primary school friends in the 1940s. We wondered if any child lived in surroundings as nice as the illustrations and decided they didn't exist. It was all make-believe, like a fairy story! I owned one book, a story book by Enid Blyton. I read it so often I practically knew the stories off by heart. In 1944, Auntie Sally gave me a lovely book about monkeys. I was delighted. I thought it was very funny and I loved the brightly coloured illustrations. Unfortunately, my wee sister was being potty trained at the time; Mum gave her my book to read, and wee sister tore it up and wiped her backside on it. I don't think I've ever completely forgiven her!

2

Transport

Joe Furphy, a Finaghy resident who spent the first thirty years of his life living on the Castlewellan Road in the town, was born in 1937. He recalls vivid memories of transport during and after the war. What he has to say applies to the whole province and I have similar memories when living in Belfast, with one important difference. Belfast had four types of public transport: trains, trams, trolley buses and petrol buses. The majority of buses were double-deckers. You had to be very careful when cycling not to get a wheel caught in the tram lines.

Joe writes, 'In wartime most people moved around the town and countryside on Shank's mare (or pony if you were a child!) – yes, walking was the normal way, usually carrying a gas mask. Not only did my mother walk into town every day (in some years wheeling a pram) to go shopping (fridges not being normal), visits to her siblings in Doughery or Ballycross were also, usually, on foot. My mother would take my brother and I for a walk most afternoons – even going as far as Ballievey, where we could watch the soldiers exercising in the fields on the opposite side of the river. Sunday afternoons saw many townsfolk heading into the countryside around the town for a good post-dinner walk.

'Bicycles were everywhere – all shapes and sizes – almost all were black. Almost everyone had, or had ready access to, a bicycle. Even professional folk used them going to and from work – Dr Crowe, headmaster of the Academy, cycled from Ballievey House to school every day – even he did not have a car until the early 1950s. Ladies' bikes were surprisingly open in construction – one of these was called the 'Daisy Bell' – of a fairly tall and long construction. Men's machines all had crossbars; to obviate the need to throw one's leg over it, some had a short bar sticking out from each side of the rear axle, allowing the rider to mount from the back – I thought this was even more precarious than the traditional way, but perhaps it helped some people with injured backs. A very few locals – other than children – had tricycles. As the owner of a (hand-me-down) 1935-built machine, I can state that the weight of these things was massive compared with the lightweight, superbly balanced examples of today. To suffer a puncture, especially on country roads and lanes, was a regular hazard. In Belfast tram lines were a hazard for cyclists because it was very easy to get stuck in them.

'For many country dwellers, the main transport was a horse- or pony-drawn trap or cart. Many businesses also used horses – milkmen and bread servers being the most familiar. The carts were surprisingly tall and the bread server had to sit up high on the top – surely a precarious position! My father earned a mention in the *Chronicle* after catching a runaway horse and bread van at the bottom of Bridge Street. It had broken away from Bob McCagherty while he was at a house at the bottom of the Castlewellan Road! I also remember a man from The Montiaghs [an area near Portadown] coming round with a cart laden with peat – surely a long trip just to make a few shillings. Indeed, on a winter evening he would leave for his 15-mile drive, having first lit his lamps – which were probably candle-powered rather than paraffin!'

Pony and trap. (Printed with kind permission of Florence Chambers)

Motor Vehicles

I moved to Banbridge in 1975. Until well into the 1980s a couple of delight-ful men used to appear several times a year and sell peat (turf). It was excellent quality, they said they'd dug it out of their land in the Montiaghs and it was reasonably priced, so we bought it. I presume it was the same family described by Joe. Their horse and cart had been replaced by a dilapidated lorry with brakes that must have been dodgy because when they parked it on the steep hill outside my house they were always careful to point its wheels at the hedge and stick a rock under them. We loved burning peat and were sorry when they stopped delivering it. On Ballymoney Hill we had a lemonade man and a milkman until well into the '80s. (See Shopping.)

Before, during and after the Second World War there was no restriction on the type of car on the road, or who was driving. No MOTs, no driving tests, no breathalysers, no seat belts, no indicators (you stuck your arm out the window and did hand signals). Cars had poor headlights and individual windscreen wipers for the driver and the front-seat passenger!

You had to have a driving licence, they were introduced in 1935, but you didn't have to do a test to prove you could drive it! I, in common with most others of my vintage, have a driving licence and I've never done a driving test!

Joe Furphy recalls, 'Few people, other than major business owners and professional folk, had cars. Most of the cars were pre-war; three in particular stand out in my mind – the elegant Bentley of the Anderson family (with its chauffeur, Hugh Downey), the beautiful Riley of the solicitor Mr R.S. Heron (IJ 612) and, the cream of all, the 1920s Morris owned by the Cowdy family. We had an Austin 7 – CZ 3637 – which was hardly ever used because of the severe petrol rationing. Many people used taxis for longer trips – Messrs Porter and Kane, Gerry Fitzpatrick, William Bell and Billy Grafton among the operators. While few businesses had vans or lorries, these were not common until several years after 1945.'

My father, the late **Bill Henry**, told me about his friend, the late **Sam McKelvey**'s experiences with his first car. Sam bought it, was shown how to turn the ignition on, use the accelerator and brake and how to change gear. Armed with that scant knowledge and filled with pride, he took his new car to attend a funeral. In those days a funeral service was held either in a church or at the home of the deceased. Then four men carried the coffin along the street, followed by a solemn procession of smartly dressed men wearing suits, shirts

Sam McKelvey.

and ties and coats if it was cold or wet. Cars drove slowly behind the men and at some point the coffin would be placed in the hearse and the men either got into a private car or one of the limousines hired for the occasion. Then the procession proceeded to the cemetery, unless of course the cemetery was comparatively near, in which case men took it turns to carry the coffin there. Each turn was called 'a lift'. The closest male relatives took the first lift, followed by more distant relatives and good friends. (Women didn't take part in a funeral procession. They stayed at home and prepared a meal for the men when they'd returned from the interment.) The service Sam attended was held on the Antrim Road and the body was interred a considerable distance away in Dundonald Cemetery.

In those days changing car gears was a complicated process. You had to 'double de-clutch'. In other words, you had to manually match the speed of the car's engine to the speed of its wheels. When changing up through the gears you listened to the sound of the engine. When it began to whine you took the car out of gear, listened until the engine speed matched the speed of the wheels, and replaced the clutch in gear. You also had to judge engine speed when changing down. That took a considerable amount of practice!

Sam was very pleased with himself. He wasn't dependant on a hired limousine. He had his own transport! He got to the service in style, joined the procession and drove behind the processing men in an orderly fashion. Dundonald Cemetery is several miles from the Antrim Road, so the body was eventually placed in the hearse and the procession of cars set out for Dundonald. All went well until they were in the centre of Belfast passing the City Hall. Sam stalled the engine when changing gear. He couldn't get it going again and caused mayhem!

When I was a student in the late '50s nine of us squashed into an Austin Mini. I was the third row in the back seat! We were spotted by the policeman on points duty in Shaftesbury Square, Belfast. He laughed and waved us on!

Before, during and after the war, nearly all cars were black. You didn't have much of a choice regarding colour, although there was the very occasional dark green or maroon car. Colour choice became possible in the '50s and my father bought a pale turquoise Austin 35. It was a small car and when we went out in it it practically stopped the traffic as people gathered round it every time we had to stop at traffic lights, or a crossroads. Mum said she felt like the Queen, except people were looking at the car and not her!

Railway Travel

Joe Furphy has a lifelong passion for all things railway related. He writes, 'Trains to Belfast, Newcastle and Scarva operated throughout the war period; steam haulage was universal except on the Scarva line, where the pioneer "A" diesel had entered service in 1932, followed a year later by "B", which was the first diesel–electric railcar to operate in the British Isles. They could be driven from either end; I remember once my mother accidentally blocked the exit for the driver with a pram and didn't notice the driver's frantic waves through the little window in the door! Traffic was generally heavy on all routes. I remember being awakened in the middle of the night by trains carrying troops destined for camps at Castlewellan or Ballykinlar. These were long and heavy, but because of weight restrictions on the line, no large locomotives could be used, and as double-heading was out of the question, it was hard work for locomotives and crews on the long inclines! While at school I befriended a local signalman and was able to try my hand at controlling the local lines from the railway worker's signal cabin, and we had the type of interesting experiences "health and safety" would prohibit today!

'While attending Banbridge Academy I struck up a friendship with a chap called **Donald Rodgers**, and soon discovered that his father, Jack, was the stationmaster. We began to visit the station regularly on Sunday afternoons, when only one train was due to arrive from Belfast and the signalman was the only member of staff on duty.

'There was plenty to occupy and interest us – particularly in the engine shed. There we would climb into the cabs of both locomotives and pretend we were drivers!

'The cab controls were a confusing mixture of little wheels, varying sizes of levers and an array of gauges. We learnt that the big lever in the centre was the regulator, which controlled the amount of steam entering the cylinders, thus allowing the speed to be varied. What was also exciting was to open the smoke box door at the front of the engine. This was usually rather smelly and very grimy, despite all the best efforts of the men who had been cleaning the engine the night before.

'In the goods yard we had a good look at the wagons, without interfering with them in any way.

'One day, Donald and I had to move rolling stock – it was only a diminutive platelayer's truck, mind you, but we probably prevented a nasty collision in doing so. We had gone for a walk on the line towards Belfast when we came across a truck that some vandals had propelled out of the goods yard towards the main line. We decided to put it back in its proper place, so pushed it some yards and then hopped on to let gravity do its work.

'This truck was a platelayer's truck, designed to be assembled and taken apart quickly to allow the passage of ordinary traffic. All went well until Donald at the rear jumped off, whereupon the front end rose up and the front wheels travelled on unchecked! As a result, the truck hit the ground between the sleepers with a resounding thump, which left me feeling very sore!

Platelayer truck. (Sourced by François Vincent from *Banbridge Chronicle's* archives)

'On a rail transport system, signalling control is a vital operation. Train movements are controlled by way of railway signals and block systems from signal cabins overlooking the railway lines. This system is designed to ensure that trains operate safely, over the correct route and to the proper timetable. There were two signal cabins, the smaller – South – cabin on the Katesbridge side of the station, and the much larger North cabin, which was located between the Scarva and Belfast lines, close to the bridge over the river.

'One Sunday afternoon, Donald Rodgers and I visited the North cabin, which was near the end of the platforms. The signalman that day was **Johnny Haskins**, and from then, Sunday afternoons were often spent in the cabin when it was his turn to be on duty. He very kindly and efficiently taught me

Signal box. (Sourced by François Vincent from *Banbridge Chronicle's* archives)

many of the technical aspects of the job, which was more complicated than I had at first realised.

'First I had to learn the layout of the lines under his control. The first line to be laid to Banbridge was that to Scarva, and when the signal box was closed down at night the layout of the points reflected this.

'The line to Belfast crossed the Scarva line just outside the box; the line to Newcastle continued through the station. In the station there were parallel tracks – one for each platform – which became single tracks a short distance beyond the station. The points and signals for all these were controlled from this cabin. To help the signalman the levers were differently coloured – for the signals, for the points, for the locking bars to hold the points in place once set. Each lever was numbered, and their locations shown on a map framed and hanging in a prominent place high up over the levers. The lever No. 1 in the cabin was the most difficult to pull. The signal which it worked by a combination of levers and cables was located some distance away uphill towards Dromore and round two gentle curves. Once I had to make three attempts before it came off; no sooner had I sat down than the diesel came over the bridge and headed towards the platform – the driver had seen my first two attempts and assumed the signalman was a weakling and drove on!

'My most exciting experience was in 1955. The buses were on strike at a time when the churches had their annual excursions to coastal resorts, but the Great Northern Railway (GNR) stepped in and ran these excursions. Even though the line to Newcastle had recently been closed it was opened specially. When I reached the station, I saw that Johnny Haskins was the signalman, so cheekily I went to the cabin. Johnny suggested I should accept the train from the signalman in Dromore. I then set the points, requested the signalman at Banbridge South – just beyond the station – to accept the train.

'Once all that was done, I went back onto the platform, and when the train arrived I climbed aboard. All in all, quite a feat for a schoolboy.

'Passenger trains from Banbridge to Newcastle and Belfast were steam-hauled until the arrival of the large diesel railcars. Most carriages had six or eight compartments. Those with fewer doors and internal gangways were largely on more prestigious routes.

'By then there were two classes – first and third. The former was more spacious, with more comfortable seating, and some carriages even had photographs on the wall. Doors had drop-down windows secured internally by a leather strap. Doors could be locked externally by the guard but not

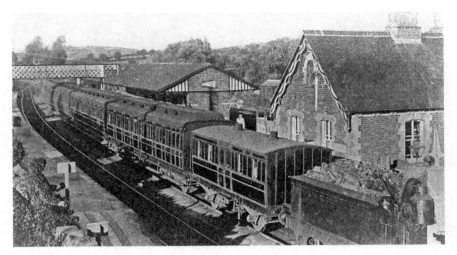

Steam train in Scarva station. (Sourced by François Vincent from *Banbridge Chronicle's* archives)

internally. Eight or ten people could be accommodated in a third-class compartment. I never had the privilege of travelling first class on a compartmentalised carriage, so I don't know how many could use it!

'Train designers were probably aware that serious competition was already lurking in the late 1940s, in the form of road transport, and there was a need to improve the design of carriages for a more comfortable passenger experience. In the late 1940s, Great Northern Railway (GNR) introduced a series of three-coach railcars, which were so much more comfortable. With fewer doors and central gangways, there was a feeling of greater space, added to which the large windows allowed the countryside to be better appreciated.

'There were twelve seats for first class at each end of the train, and with a clear view through the driving compartment it was very pleasant – I first found this to be the case when I travelled first class on the final train to Dromore!

'These diesels were a vast change to the Scarva diesels and the railbuses to which we had become accustomed. In the early 1930s, the Scarva diesels were the forerunners of diesel traction on the GNR. The railbuses were just that – road buses with the wheels replaced by railway wheels. Rattly but useful!

'All normal passenger traffic on the Scarva line was handled by diesels. Steam-hauled trains were used on 13 July for visitors to the Sham Fight, and for Thursdays-only excursion trains from Dublin to Newcastle. Magnificent

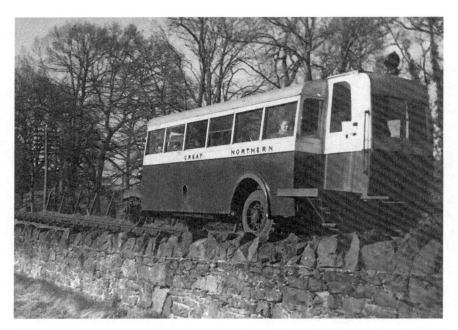

GNR Railbus at Dunbar crossing between Banbridge and Scarva. (Printed with kind permission of Joe Furphy)

Dundalk to Greenore train crossing Riverstown viaduct. (Photograph printed with kind permission of George Beattie)

though they were, steam engines were fairly dour-looking until the "powers that be" at GNR realised that they could cheer them up by painting them a colour other than black! Locos, already named after loughs, appeared in blue. Other blue locos to reach Banbridge were the 1948 County class and the Mountains, originally built for express work.

'In 1948 the GNR introduced an experimental German goods loco, which would visit Banbridge from time to time; it did once reach Katesbridge.

'To enable locos to always face forward, a turntable was sited in the goods yard. On at least two occasions derailments occurred there in normal use.'

Travel by rail was a very human experience. Stationmasters had an attractive house near the platform and took pride in their gardens. Each station had a cosy waiting room with a coal fire. Waiting rooms provided a warm pleasant place to sit. I have been told when coal was in short supply during the war people used to go and sit in railway stations. They'd no intention of going anywhere. They just enjoyed a bit of craic and the heat! The porters were helpful. When I worked staff in Wallace High School in Lisburn, **Joan Wilson**, another staff member, dropped a shoe onto the line as she got on the train. The porter instructed the driver to move the train, climbed down onto the line and retrieved her shoe!

Bus Transport

Joe Furphy records, 'The Northern Ireland Road Transport Board operated bus services on several main routes. These buses had a conductor as well as a driver. The conductor ran up and down the inside of the bus selling tickets. Because of the war, it was not always possible to operate closely to timetables and I remember some delays. We saw a variety of bus types, most with the driver housed in an enclosed cabin and with doors at the rear. Heavy luggage was stored in an open space on the roof. Because of the demand for buses for transporting factory and other workers, NIRTB had to buy buses from Britain and also build new "Utility" buses with the door at the front and the driver unenclosed. Of spartan build, they had uncompromising wooden slatted seats; thankfully, they had all gone by the end of 1947. There were no double-deckers until after the war, when they were introduced on the Portadown route; McMaster's railway bridge at Derriaghy was too low for double-deckers and indeed it was not until 1959 that we saw them on the Newry to Belfast route.

'At the end of my second year in Queen's, a fellow student told me how much he had enjoyed working the previous summer as a bus conductor in Lisburn – and this persuaded me to take up his offer to be introduced as the controller there. He arranged for the appropriate medical tests and so on. Just after lectures finished, I was posted to Lisburn, where not only did I have to learn the location of many unfamiliar places, but also had to get used, quickly, to simple tasks like opening the doors, adjusting the settings on the ticket-issuing machine (a heavy and cumbersome instrument), learning the bell codes (one pull on the chain for go, two to stop, four for an emergency stop), learning the names of every stop on each route, trying to remember the fare lists, entering the details of tickets sold on my waybill, etc.

'Meanwhile, in Banbridge I was accepted as part of the team and made many friends among the crews, several of whom I had already come across while travelling to Queen's. Some guys really stood out as characters – including **Tommy O'Hanlon**, nicknamed 'Keady' because that was his birthplace. When front-door buses were introduced, passengers were regularly entertained when he forgot that the whole bus could hear his comments on other road users, traffic lights that were slow to respond and many other aspects! After the introduction of double-deckers in 1959 (following the replacement of McMaster's Bridge at Derriaghy) all buses were prohibited from driving through 'The Cut' but had to travel via Victoria Street and Scarva Street before reaching Newry Street across the top of the bridge. One day soon after this rerouting took place, driver Joe Burns left the depot (then in an office beside Bell's public house) on his bicycle to go home for lunch. After a few yards, he came back and asked, in a jocular manner, was he still allowed to cycle through 'The Cut' while wearing uniform! I remember **Jack Lacey** (see Chapter 9) being challenged to bring a double-decker from Hillsborough to Banbridge in twenty minutes – and he succeeded!

'Most of the main routes from Banbridge still exist, but in those days there were also services to Rathfriland by three routes, to Newcastle, to Hill's Cross Roads, to take mill workers at Ballievey out and back, plus a variety of school runs to outlying areas.

'In those days several drivers had first been conductors, like **Bobby Adair**, **Tom McGrath** and **Will Currie**; one whose first passenger-carrying trip I was on was **Eric McDowell**. He drove the 6.15 a.m. double-decker from Banbridge to Belfast – covering all stops. Most of the passengers on that service were men working in Harland and Wolff's shipyard or the aircraft factory. The craic was great and it was a good service to be on – for me, it allowed me to get to the depot in Lisburn in time to start my 7.15 shift. To say I greatly enjoyed my time on the buses is an understatement – I learnt so much about human nature in so many aspects, benefited from great companionship, earned enough money to buy my first camera (even on £7 7s 6d in old money per week) and, I hope, made me into a more rounded person! I even learnt (without authority) how to drive and park a double-decker!'

3

Industries in the Province Before, During and After the Second World War

Manufacturing facilities

Harland and Wolff was one of the largest shipbuilding yards in the world. It had constructed many ships for the White Star Line like RMS *Titanic* and RMS *Olympic*, and for the Royal Navy, including aircraft carriers such as HMS *Formidable* and *Unicorn*, the cruisers HMS *Belfast* and *Penelope*, as well as 131 other naval vessels. Up to 35,000 people were employed.

During the war years, Belfast shipyards built or converted over 3,000 Navy vessels, repaired more than 22,000 others and launched over half a million tons of merchant shipping – over 140 merchantmen.

Short Brothers manufactured aircraft. They are best known for the Sunderland flying boat and the Stirling long-range heavy bomber. Up to 20,000 people were employed. The factory was re-equipping as early as 1936 for the manufacture of 189 Handley Page Hereford bombers.

James Mackie & Sons were re-equipped in 1938. They were the primary supplier of Bofors anti-aircraft shells.

Harland's Engineering works built tanks. They designed the Churchill.

Belleek factory, 1941, Parian ware. (Photograph by Bill Henry)

Belleek factory, 1941. Parian ware in the foreground, utility pottery produced for the war effort in the background. (Photograph by Bill Henry)

Aero linen for covering aircraft, such as the Hawker Hurricane, and military glider frames, was manufactured by a number of Belfast flax spinning mills, such as The York Street Flax Spinning Co.; Brookfield Spinning Co.; Wm. Ewart's Rosebank Weaving Co.; and the Linen Thread Co.

Other Belfast factories manufactured gun mountings, ordnance pieces, aircraft parts and ammunition.

Factories outside Belfast were repurposed to manufacture goods for the war effort. Considerations of space do not allow all of them to be discussed, apart from two examples: the parachute factory in Carrickfergus and the aircraft manufacturing factory in Banbridge. Linen factories were repurposed to make Army, Navy and Air Force uniforms and the Belleek factory in County Fermanagh changed from making ornamental Parian ware to everyday pottery.

War materials and food were sent by sea from Belfast to Britain, some under the protection of the neutral Irish tricolour, the national flag of what was then the Irish Free State. The MV *Munster*, for example, operated by the Belfast Steamship Company, plied between Belfast and Liverpool under the tricolour, until she hit a mine and was sunk outside Liverpool.

Manufacture of Parachutes

Adrian Hack, who organises very interesting walking tours around Carrickfergus, writes, 'My mother-in-law as a young woman assembled parachutes in a factory in Carrickfergus, a small town 10 miles north-east of Belfast that was developed to meet the needs of the war effort. Factories were repurposed to build tanks, assemble uniforms, supply webbing used as belts and straps by the Army, and one became a military prison. Most interestingly, to me anyway, one particular firm became the largest parachute factory in the world at the time of it opening.

'Barn Mills, on the outskirts of the town, was built in the 1790s as a cotton mill. In the middle of the nineteenth century it adapted to be part of the burgeoning linen industry developing within Northern Ireland.

'In the early years of the Second World War, the government commissioned reports on the viability of converting existing manufacturing businesses into ones that could support the needs of the military. Barn Mills was identified as one such factory, and in 1942 the Littlewoods Company, based in the North of England, took over the company and began work on repurposing the building, retraining its existing workforce and recruiting new machinists. The town of Carrickfergus had a population of just 4,500 at this stage, so the factory relied on women from the surrounding area to come to Carrickfergus and work there.

'Within twelve months, more than 1,000 people, mainly women, were working in the factory, initially producing parachutes. It took six women to make each parachute: one to cut the material (silk, and later a silk/polyester mix) from a pattern; an assembler, who loosely stitched the component parts together; a stitcher, who put double seams down each join; harnesses and cables were attached; a packer folded the parachute in a specific manner and put it into the 'chute pack'; and finally a supervisor ensured quality control. Each group of six women was expected to create a minimum of four parachutes per day, with the more experienced ones able to produce six or seven a day. With the necessary skills and logistics developed, the factory took on other projects. A small number of large helium balloons, used for target practice by anti-aircraft crews, were made, followed by a significant number of Mae West life jackets.

'From late 1943 to mid-1944, some of the factory girls worked, in secret, to make para-dummies. These were cloth 'dolls' that, from a distance, resembled the outline of a paratrooper. Later, these had small explosives added to them, and were dropped from aircraft using miniature parachutes. They were used as part of Operation Titanic, a distraction exercise, on D-Day, 6 June 1944.

'In the hours immediately before the beach landings in Normandy, thousands of these para-dummies (nicknamed 'Rupert', a name used by enlisted men for their posh senior officers) were airlifted above forests a few miles inland. As they dropped, they were identified from the ground as being a large paratrooper assault, just as intended. On contact with the ground, the small explosives went off, not to cause harm but to sound like grenades. The effect, in early dawn, was realistic enough that thousands of German troops rushed to defend against the 'airborne assault', reducing the effectiveness of the beach defences.

'There is no doubt that the hard work of the women back in Barn Mills had helped save countless lives on the Longest Day.'

Agriculture

The productivity of farms increased enormously during the war to meet the increased demand for food. The United Kingdom, then like now, was not self-sufficient and the action of German U-boats made importing food hazardous. Local farmers responded magnificently. (See table below. Extrapolated from J. W. Blake's book, *Northern Ireland in the Second World War*.)

Year	1939	1940	1945
oats	270 tons	378 tons	383 tons
potatoes	864 tons	1,030 tons	1,089 tons
flax	4.5 tons	8.7 tons	14.2 tons
wheat	3 tons	13 tons	2 tons
barley	3 tons	15 tons	12 tons
mixed corn	0.4 tons	4.3 tons	6.3 tons

George Wilson, who lives, and lived, at Ballydugan, remembers working on his family farm during the war. He records, 'There was little difference in farming practices between the years 1840 and 1940 but unbelievable changes have occurred beginning in the early 1950s. Before, during and immediately after the war most farm labour was done by men and horses, with an occasional old Fordson tractor, which Henry Ford had sent to Britain. Things began to change during the war, when Harry Ferguson, who was born near Dromore, County Down, started mass producing tractors. The Ferguson tractor transformed farming in the 1950s.

'In 1940 there were about 130,000 horses and few tractors. A one-furrow horse ploughed an acre of land in a day and the farmer walked approximately 13 miles. In 1944 there were 6,789 tractors in Northern Ireland and in 1945 the number of horses had gone down to 81,745. In 1951 a tractor

Free range hens on a farm near Five Mile Town in 1941. (Photograph by Bill Henry)

with a two-furrow plough could plough between 5 and 6 acres a day, the farmer didn't have to walk and he lost the close relationship he had with his horses. That trend has continued while farms have increased in size.

'We became an accredited poultry farm with twenty hens and a rooster, so our eggs could be sent to a hatchery.

'One of the best things we did was buy an incubator. It turned eggs over automatically and all we had to do was sprinkle them with water. It was exciting to see the chicks break out of the shell. We kept the hens and ate the roosters. The best-paid job was that of a chicken sexer, but that came later. We didn't know which was which until the birds started to mature! The ratio would have been about fifty hens to fifty roosters. We also hatched ducks.

'We got a petrol Ferguson in 1949 costing £370, a plough was £50. We then got a Ferguson Power Take Off cutting bar at £80. During the 1950s we mowed around 200 acres for twenty-five local small farmers each year. Haymaking was done mainly with a fork and rake. People only wanted about 2 acres cut at a time and it took all summer to make 10 to 20 acres of hay. I remember good long summers then.

Scythe.

'When we made hay in the 1950s it took us an hour to cut 2 acres. Now a machine can do it in five minutes.

'In the old days the hay would have been cut in swathes. We used a cutting bar and a scythe was used to cut round ditches. The grass was let lie for a couple of days to dry, after which it was turned with a fork and left until it was dry enough to be built into a rick (hut). It's very important for the hay to be dried properly to keep it from fermenting. The next stage was to build it up into a 5 to 6ft-tall stack. They stayed in the fields all summer before being moved to the farm yard. If you had a barn to store your hay until it was used you were landed! If there was a strong wind it could tumble the hay stack and it'd have to be rebuilt and a hay shed prevented that. There's hardly any hay made now and all the hay sheds are lying derelict.

'I think that climate change has caused wet summers that don't allow for haymaking and the big black round bales are a Godsend for farmers. Now we can do what used to be a month's work in a few days.

'The unbelievable progress in farming is sad in one way because farming has become less sociable. Neighbours used to help each other to bring in the hay, so on my farm there could have been twenty-six people working in a field and the craic was mighty. Today there's only one person and farming has become a lonely job!

'Corn and barley were cut by a mowing machine, then came the binder, which was a great machine but there was a lot of hard labour storing and building ricks of corn, carting it to the farmyard and building big stacks.'

Growing Flax and Preparing Flax for the Production of Linen

The Second World War effort gave a boost to the linen industry, which was once huge, employing more than 70,000 people. Practically every town and village in Northern Ireland had a factory, either producing thread such as Dunbar McMaster, in Gilford, which was taken over by Barbour Threads, or a weaving factory such as Ferguson Factory in Banbridge. Many places had both types of factory. Ten years after the war in 1955 there were fifty-five linen spinners in Northern Ireland. The last one closed in 2009. Ferguson's factory, in Banbridge, is the last weaving factory of any substantial size. There used to be thirty-eight in Banbridge alone.

Linen production begins by growing flax. Ballydougan resident **George Wilson** recalls with great fondness how farming life once revolved around the precious crop.

The linen produced from flax was not just used to make clothes, sheets and thread – it was central to the war effort, since the tails of the Lancaster bombers and Spitfires were covered in it.

George, who was born on 15 April 1939, was a very young boy during the war, however he vividly remembers those busy war years when his farming community, ably assisted by the Land Army ladies, helped produce linen fibre of the highest quality.

Eugene McConville using a seed fiddle.

George recalls, 'Flax was a very labour intensive crop, both to grow and to prepare. The ground was relatively weed free because it had been carefully prepared. The seeds were placed close together, broadcast or using a seed fiddle so that the plants grew straight without any useless side branches. The young plants were weeded when the crop was about 9in high. Harvest was about fourteen weeks after it was sown, that is, about three or four weeks after the first blossoms appeared. The blossoms turned the fields blue and the country-side became even more beautiful than usual.

'Farmers needed a great deal of expertise to tell exactly when the crop was ready. If it was pulled too soon the fibres were weak and useless, if pulled too late they were too thick to be made into fine linen. It is impossible to produce both useful fibres and seeds on the same plant. The best fibres for turning into threads are found in plants with immature seeds that can't germinate. The fibres of plants with mature seeds were so thick they couldn't be used to produce linen.

'The fibres inside the plant go right down to the roots, so flax was harvested by being pulled out by the roots by hand until well into the 1940s. Harvesters pulled the plant upwards and slightly to one side. Four handfuls of flax made a "beet" or sheaf, which were tied with rushes. Then the beets were pulled through a rippling comb, made from a plank that had a set of 10in (25cm) nails driven into it and supported above the ground, sometimes in the back of a cart. That meant the immature seeds fell into the cart and were used as animal fodder, or to make linseed oil.

'After the flax had been cut and tied into beets with rushes (string or rope would have rotted in water) it was ready for the next process, which was retting, that is being placed in a flax dam (lint hole) under water so the plant rotted, leaving the fibres free.'

Flax beets.

'Farmers always helped each other to harvest crops. During the war there was added pressure to produce the maximum amount possible. Many men were away fighting and the Women's Land Army was formed in 1941 to fill the gap. The women did all sorts of jobs, such as harvesting, planting, weeding crops, catching rats and so on. Every job a man could do could be done by a land girl, as the women came to be called.

'Land girls came from all over the country, including towns and cities, and could either live on a farm or be put up in a hostel. They usually worked hard and did an excellent job, although they were paid less than men were for the same job. They were cheap to hire because the government subsidised their wages.

'I remember in 1944, when I was 5, a squad of land girls came to our farm. They ranged in age from 18 to 50 years. One of the girls was a real beauty. She was aged about 20 and she had her mother with her. The mother was fat and jolly. She was set at the far corner of the field to work while the girl worked alongside one of our boys. It was obvious that the pair fancied each other. They were laughing and giggling together.

'I was with my dad and uncle in a small lorry, bringing beets from the field to the flax dam to ret. When we came back from the flax dam the young couple were lying in a corner of the field. I wondered what they were doing? They certainly weren't pulling flax!

'Harvesters were paid for the number of beets they'd produced. You should have heard the tonguing that girl got at the end of the day. I can hear her mother screaming yet when she discovered how little her daughter'd earned!

'Our flax dam like a small swimming pool was at the bottom of a field. It was about 3m wide and 7 or 8m long, filled with water from the drain and sealed. All 3 acres of flax grown on our farm were put in the hole and kept down under the water by big stones or cement blocks for about two weeks, depending on the weather.'

Sometimes flax dams ran along beside roads. The late **John Campbell**, a storyteller from South Armagh, described running along on top of the stones holding flax down. He said, 'When we jumped on the stones great bubbles of stinking gas, the kind small boys love, came up to the surface and we set it alight. The flame produced wasn't very hot so we were able to run along on flaming water! It was fun! The farmers didn't mind us doing that. It must have helped with the retting process.'

George Wilson writes, 'Flax was left under water for about two or three weeks until it was ready to be taken out and dried. If it was taken out either too early or too late the crop was destroyed, so farmers needed a lot of expertise to decide when to open the flax dam. The opening process made the whole countryside around it stink to high heaven. The smell, like that of a skunk, clung to skin and clothes and it was impossible to get rid of it for several weeks.

'Unfortunately men were expected to get into the flax dam to lift the beets out. Only old men, or very young boys, were willing to do that! There was a farmer who lived near us who used to take all his clothes off and jump, naked, into the flax dam! My father was crafty. He used to stick a ladder into the dam and stand on that. He was able to throw the beets onto the bank using a pitchfork. He only got his feet wet, and my mother? Well, she was married to him so she just had to put up with the smell of them until it wore off!

'Once it was taken out of the dam the beets were opened out to dry before being carted into the farmyard and built into stacks to wait their turn to be taken to the scutch mill to undergo the next stage in the process. If you paid your scutch mill owner's bill quickly, waiting was kept to a minimum. There was a saying, "Short accounts mean long friends."'

Scutch Mills

Scutching was a dangerous process in which unwanted dried parts of the plant were knocked off the linen fibres. The flax was 'bruised' by being run through wooden rollers to make stiff dried plants pliable and loosen and remove unwanted plant parts. Then the flax was taken over to a wooden post, or 'stock', and hit with a blunt wooden blade. This knocked the unwanted parts of the plant off, leaving the phloem fibres which formed linen threads. The fibres were hackled by being put through a hackling comb to make sure they were all lying the same way. Spinning turns short fibres into a long yarn.

A scutch mill's air became clouded with highly flammable dust, so mills frequently burnt down. The dust got into workers' lungs and aggravated any tendency to suffer lung disease.

Eugene scutching.

The waste left over from scutching was called 'chowes'. It was collected by the poor and used for the stuffing of things such as mattresses.

Wages were very low. Men worked at the loom for fourteen hours a day for a net income of 4*s* a day, or less.

Spinning Mills

The majority of workers in a spinning mill were women. Men were only employed to service machinery and act as managers.

Nora Bates was born in Saintfield and in her book *Up the Down Street* described working during the 1940s in the mill in Comber owned by **John Andrews**. She recorded that the nature of the work meant windows couldn't be opened. She said the air was dry and full of dust, and sometimes she was sent to work in one of the rooms where she had to stand, barefoot, in water all day. She was a 'spreader' when she started working in the mill. The flax threads came along on a conveyer belt. She made sure they were straight before they disappeared into a tunnel at the end of the room, after which they passed to the doffers to be spun into thread.

'Doff' means to remove. Machines spun yarn from a large bobbin or spindle, twisting the flax fibres into a thread. When the spindles ran out of yarn doffers replaced them with new ones. When the threads were spun they were loaded onto huge bobbins before being woven into cloth. The work was dangerous because bobbins and shuttlecocks could fly unexpectedly around the room, causing serious injury.

Cowdy's Mill, in Banbridge, had such a terrible reputation for death and injury during the 1950s it was referred to locally as Belsen. Nobody ever got any compensation because the owners always argued the worker had been in the wrong place at the time.

Thread had to be kept in a moist atmosphere during the first stages of manufacture, so the girls working there worked in their bare feet. That was preferable to destroying shoes, which were expensive. I used to see mill girls going to work during the '50s, when I was sitting on a bus travelling across the city to go to the Methodist College (Methody). I felt heart sorry for them as they hurried along Castlereagh Street on frosty mornings, their feet purple with cold, wrapped in shawls, hence their nickname, 'shawlies', so badly paid they couldn't afford coats.

As the threads moved up the mill, becoming finer and finer at every level, the conditions became more pleasant. It was no longer necessary to stand in water all day.

The doffers were usually young girls and they were under the charge of a doffing mistress, known as the 'Tidy Doffer'. There was a lot of camaraderie between the workers and they used to sing a variety of songs, such as 'The Tidy Doffer' or 'The Doffing Mistress' (see below), as they worked.

The Doffing Mistress

Oh do you know her or do you not
This new doffing mistress we have got
Elsie Thompson★ is her name
And she helps her doffers at every frame
Chorus (repeated after every verse)
Fol de ri fol ra
Fol de ri fol ray
She hangs her coat on the highest pin
Sometimes the boss he looks in the door
'Tie up your ends' he will roar
Tie up our ends we surely do
For Elsie Thompson but not for you.

★ the girls would have substituted the name of their own doffing mistress for Elsie Thompson.

Weaving and Finishing the Linen

Marion McDowell worked in Ferguson's factory as a damask weaver. Today Ferguson's supplies a wide range of organisations from designers at London Fashion Week, the furnishing industry under their John England brand, to film and TV productions. They embroider on-site badges for, among others, the Scouts and Girl Guides under their Franklins brand. If you visit any gift shop in Northern Ireland you will find Irish linen products made by Thomas Ferguson and if you have ever watched *Game of Thrones* you would have seen fabrics woven at the Ferguson factory. The factory worked very closely with the TV show's costume department to create fabrics for its costumes. Linen has the perfect properties for TV because it can look old and worn when it is creased and brand new again once it is washed and ironed. During the Second World War they produced uniforms for the military.

Marion says, 'I loved working in Ferguson's factory. The owners were very caring. Mills and factories could be dangerous places, shuttles could fly off or you could get caught in the side of the loom. Ferguson's employed every safety device possible. They had belts covering the sides of looms, so you couldn't become trapped in them. It was very noisy, so we used to communicate with our fingers, signalling to each other when we were going to have our breaks and so on. We had great craic. We used to play jokes on young apprentice boys, like asking them to go and fetch a "bucket of steam", or find us a "rubber hammer".

'I was a damask weaver. That's the most highly skilled job. You have to watch a lot of things. You have a card, with the pattern on it held above the loom. Lots of things could go wrong and there were stoppers on the loom, so if a thread broke the loom would stop. We were paid by piece work and clocks registered the work you'd done. Once a piece of work was finished it went to the office to be inspected. You were fined if it had more than three faults.

'I'd been working in Ferguson's for some time when new looms were installed. They were more efficient and not as noisy as the old ones, but they still made a heck of a clatter. Of course, the weaver had to learn how to handle the new looms. I started off with two looms and ended up looking after ten! I had a lot of running up and down to do as there were many things that could go wrong. I had to keep checking the cards. I found altar cloths lovely things to weave. We also made tablecloths and napkins for the

Royal family's big occasions, such as the Coronation and royal weddings. Today their linen is sent to heads of state throughout the world.'

Linen is brown, so in the past Ferguson's sent it to Bellievey Mill to be bleached and possibly dyed. There it was spread out on the fields to be turned white by the sun before being made up. Bellievey Mill was also responsible for sewing the cloth into its intended end product. The girls who worked there were always very well dressed and they wore hats. According to company representative **Neil Spiers**, 'The factory workers thought the girls working at Bellievey were "stuck up" and wouldn't speak them! I don't know all the details but I was told a woman, who in the distant past worked in the linen industry, got very annoyed about the way she was treated so she put a curse on the River Bann. She prophesied, "There'll be no more factories or mills on the Bann in 100 years' time!" They've all gone. Even Ferguson's, the last survivor, is not situated on the Bann. It has moved to the Scarva Road.'

The countryside in Northern Ireland has changed beyond recognition since the war. Fields that once had sheets of linen bleaching in the sun are now covered in houses.

My Auntie **Carrie Husband** (see Chapters 1 and 4) was a seamstress in a Belfast factory (unfortunately I don't know which one) and told me the boys used to play tricks on the girls, including putting some sort of chemical in their tea that turned their urine blue. She was paid by piece work. When she finished a piece of sewing it had to be taken to the office to be inspected, where it was held up against a door frame and if one stitch was out of line she was fined.

Manufacture of the Miles Messenger Aeroplane

Jason Diamond, the Heritage Officer for Armagh, Banbridge and Craigavon Council (commonly called the ABC Council), writes: 'There are a few stories that come to mind about the linen industry during the Second World War. Like many factories during that time, production was given over to the manufacture of munitions.

'The late **Billy Fiyvie** was a wealth of knowledge on the history of Banbridge but he surprised me one day when he told me that he used to work in the aeroplane factory in Banbridge. "Hold on Billy, there was an aeroplane factory in Banbridge!?" Billy then related to me the history of the Miles Aircraft factory, which was set up in the town in 1943 in what had been the old Walker's linen factory on the Castlewellan Road (some of the buildings can still be seen as you cross over the suspension bridge in Solitude Park towards the Castlewellan Road).

'The old factory was converted for the task by Messrs John Graham of Dromore and initial production concentrated on the manufacture of "monoplane air tails" used on air-launched torpedoes.

'After the success of this endeavour it was decided that Banbridge would be ideal to produce the Miles Messenger aeroplane. This was a monoplane with a 30ft wingspan, designed to carry four people and able to take off on unprepared ground.

'The aeroplane was of all wood construction, made from Canadian silver spruce and birch plywood. The factory in Banbridge was visited by **Sir Stafford Cripps**, a former ambassador to Russia and Minister of Aircraft Production, who gave a talk to the entire workforce, after which a tea party was held on the factory lawn. There is a photograph of one of these aeroplanes in the Banbridge Civic building, which was presented by Billy. The plane depicted is painted in the livery of **Field Marshal Montgomery**, who had one of these planes for his personal use.'

The late **Tommy McMaster** worked in Walkers old linen factory when it was repurposed to make planes and recorded it was very difficult to build a plane in the factory because the presence of lots of supporting columns meant the fuselage had to be threaded in and out through them. The planes could not be completely assembled on site, so they were taken to RAF Long Kesh airfield, near Hillsborough, to be assembled and undergo test flights.

4

Preparations for War

The government of Northern Ireland lacked the will, energy and capacity to cope with a major crisis when it came. James Craig, Lord Craigavon, had been Prime Minister of Northern Ireland since its inception in 1921 up until his death in 1940. His death (along with preceding ill health) came at a bad time and arguably inadvertently caused a leadership vacuum. Richard Dawson Bates was the Home Affairs Minister. Sir Basil Brooke, the Minister of Agriculture, was the only active minister. He successfully busied himself with the task of making Northern Ireland a major supplier of food to Britain in her time of need.

John Clarke MacDermott, the Minister of Public Security, after the first bombing, initiated the 'Hiram Plan' to evacuate the city and to return Belfast to 'normality' as quickly as possible. It was MacDermott who sent a telegram to de Valera seeking assistance. There was unease with the complacent attitude of the government, which led to multiple resignations.

John Edmond Warnock, the Parliamentary Secretary at the Ministry of Home Affairs, resigned from the government on 25 May 1940. He said, 'I have heard speeches about Ulster pulling her weight, but they have never carried conviction,' and 'the government has been slack, dilatory and apathetic'.

Lieutenant Colonel Alexander Gordon, Parliamentary and Financial Secretary at the Ministry of Finance (i.e. Chief Whip), resigned on 13 June 1940, explaining to the Commons that the government was 'quite unfitted to sustain the people in the ordeal we have to face'.

Craigavon died on 24 November 1940. He was succeeded by John Miller Andrews, then 69 years old, who was no more capable of dealing with the situation than his predecessor. On 28 April 1943, six members of the government threatened to resign, forcing him from office. He was replaced by 54-year-old Sir Basil Brooke on 1 May.

There was little preparation for the conflict with Germany. However, at the time Lord Craigavon said: 'Ulster is ready when we get the word and always will be.' He was asked in the N.I. parliament, 'if the government realised that these fast bombers can come to Northern Ireland in two- and three-quarter hours'. His reply was: 'We here today are in a state of war and we are prepared with the rest of the United Kingdom and Empire to face all the responsibilities that imposes on the Ulster people. There is no slacking in our loyalty.'

Dawson Bates, the Home Affairs Minister, apparently refused to reply to Army correspondence and when the Ministry of Home Affairs was informed by Imperial defence experts in 1939 that Belfast was regarded as 'a very definite German objective', little was done outside providing shelters in the harbour area.

Barbed Wire

The government expected any attack on Ireland to come from either the land border with the South or from the sea, so the border between North and South was well guarded and the shoreline was covered in barbed wire. As far as my family was concerned, that meant we could no longer go camping in the sand dunes at the White Rocks, near Portrush.

Camping at White Rocks. (Photograph by Bill Henry)

The B-Specials (Special Police Force)

The trouble caused by the IRA before and after partition resulted in 1921 in the government setting up a special police force, known as the B-Specials, to work on a part-time basis and augment normal policing. Some of its members had had bad experiences and some were bully boys. As a result they earned a bad reputation. Protestants and Catholics dreaded being stopped by the B-Specials in case they met one of the bully boys, who didn't care if they damaged you or your property, or both.

Garnet Chambers records, 'My father was a member of the B-specials and for a time of the Home Guard, which was formed when a number of experienced members of the B-specials were transferred to the new force. This was to give it a core of men used to drill and weapons training until its recruitment brought it up to required strength. The B-specials thus affected could then return or remain in the Home Guard. One of my uncles was in a similar position. In their daily work both men were professional garden-

Garnet Chambers' parents. (Printed with kind permission of Garnet Chambers)

ers and had large gardens at home. At that time we lived in Tullyear (now the Bannview Road) just about where the bypass goes underneath. One night in what must have been September 1940 they were not out on patrol and my uncle had been helping my father with something or other in the garden. It was getting dark, the oil lamp was lit and they were sitting at the fire, the Modern Mistress range, before my uncle went home. My mother was darning socks. My father and uncle were discussing the situation and my uncle gloomily thought that it looked that the Germans were going to win. My father had the opposite opinion and they were going over the pros and cons. My mother, who had taken no part in the chat, eventually put her darning in the sewing basket, stood up, pushed the kettle over the fire to make supper and said very firmly, "Hitler won't win, Mr Churchill won't let him." That settled the matter.'

Dr Vivien Gotto (1921–2006) was a brilliant, much-loved zoology lecturer at Queen's University. When I was reading zoology at Queen's University, Belfast, I had the privilege of being one of his students. He had an old banger of a car, held together by rust, its bumpers wired on and it didn't have a floor. He was very good at giving students lifts when we were on field trips. I was warned to keep my feet up and found watching the ground passing rapidly under them alarming!

Vivien was a champion tennis player. He was a member of the Irish Davis Cup team in 1953–61, captaining it on thirteen occasions. In 1953 he held both the Irish Hardcourt singles and doubles championships, and he played in five Wimbledon Championships. He used to give demonstration tennis matches with his friend, Victor Booth. He said, 'After a match with Victor on a cold wet night, I was freezing cold and soaked to the skin so, to warm up, I took my clothes off, wrapped myself up in a rug and headed towards home. I was stopped by the B-Specials. They were going to drag me out of the car, then they realised I was stark staring naked and the car hadn't a floor! I must have scared them because they got rid of me immediately!'

The Blackout

At the beginning of the war people were ordered to make sure their homes didn't show even a chink of light after dark. The headlights on cars, lorries and buses were dimmed and turned so they pointed downwards, and street lights were turned off. The white Portland stone of Stormont (Northern Ireland's seat of government) was painted black so it would not be readily identified by the Luftwaffe.

The blackout was strictly observed. Householders checked for leaking light, while the Royal Ulster Constabulary and the B–Specials helped to reinforce restrictions. The idea was to keep cities from being easily identified from the air.

Larry Breen writes, 'I was born in Lurgan in 1942, so I don't have any personal memories of what life was like in wartime Lurgan but I do remember my mum telling us about the war. She talked about the "black-out", which was double Dutch to us but mysterious enough to arouse our curiosity, so she explained that because of the real danger of bombing from German war planes there were very strict rules on keeping all domestic lights out where possible and preventing any light being visible from outside. This particularly applied to window blinds, which were a potential source of light escaping if not properly drawn. These rules were law and were bound to be kept under penalty of prosecution.

Stormont covered in black paint. (Printed with kind permission of *Belfast Telegraph*)

'People in those days were very sensitive about their good name and what their neighbours might think if they were found to have committed any misdemeanours. You can guess the consternation when one day Mum answered a knock on the door only to find a policemen standing there with a letter in his hand. It was a summons for breaking the "blackout" regulations with regard to not taking adequate precautions to prevent light being seen from the window. Apparently on one occasion our blinds were not properly drawn and light had been seen coming from the window.

'If this was not bad enough, guess the indignity when our name appeared in the local press, the *Lurgan Mail*, reporting the incident. The Breen name was in the headlines for the wrong reasons. My mum was heard to say, "We will never live this down, what will this do now to our good name."

'Another story I just loved was about "My Da" and the raspberry jam. My Da was a carpenter by trade having worked and served his time at cabinet-making, which by the way was regarded as a step up from ordinary carpentry. He served his time in McDonough's, a very reputable cabinetmaking company based in Portadown. He was what Lurgan people affectionately called a "Port-e-down" man. At the time he was working in Harland & Wolff shipyard in Belfast. One evening during the blackout he was returning home from work in the shipyard in Belfast. He travelled by train to Lurgan and this particular evening he had a surprise treat with him for Mum and the family, three jars of homemade raspberry jam, which he had kindly received from one of his workmates.

'Due to the blackout there were no lights at the railway station and to make matters worse my Da had very poor eyesight, requiring spectacles. He was very self-conscious of wearing glasses with very thick lenses in public and was therefore not wearing them at the time. He had the jars of raspberry jam in his coat pocket. Unknown to my Da, the train did not stop properly at the station platform and the last carriage, which he was in, did not reach the platform. Combining the poor light with his poor eyesight, he stepped out, missed the platform and landed on the railway track. After picking himself up, lucky not to have been killed, he discovered that he now had three broken jars of raspberry jam in his coat pockets. Mum got a surprise all right but not the one he had planned. Three broken jars of raspberry jam was her surprise.

'It is now told as a funny story but in hindsight it could have been very different, but sure all is well that ends well. So much for the surprise and the raspberry jam.'

Pat Quinn wrote in his book *Dear Little Town*, 'I remember the blackout because our toilet was in the yard outside, and I was terrified of the dark but I didn't mind its position because halfway up our stairs there was a window that gave a light into the yard. One day my mother put a large blanket up to keep the light from shining into the yard, *the blackout!* What a dirty trick! Some of my family made life hard for me by hiding in the dark and jumping out to scare me. It was not funny, so I had some reasons of my own for hating Hitler.'

Regarding the blackout, **Jay** writes, 'The world was in darkness throughout the world war. There was no mains electricity where I lived, in Ballinderry, and no lighting on roads. We had lamps indoors (oil lamps, Aladdin lamps, Tilley lamps or, rarely, candles). When visitors came to the front door, we had to carry a lamp down the hall to greet the caller. Sometimes, a tilted lamp or a sudden gust of wind made this a risky exercise. Outdoors we had hurricane lamps, carbide lamps or battery-powered torches. At Christmas, there were small red candles, fixed on metal clips, on the tree. The candles were lit for the arrival of the carol singers, who visited all the houses in the village, and blown out as soon as the singers departed, both for safety reasons and to save the precious candles for future use.

'When I was 5, I left a Sunday School party in high dudgeon because I had to take part in a game I considered foolish. I then walked home, around two sides of a graveyard and down a path in total darkness. I was too indignant to feel afraid.

'We lived in a small village, and greater dangers lurked in the dark country beyond the village. There were rumours about Skiboo, who reputedly lurked in roadside hedges to attack passing cyclists. One local lad who had a long way to cycle home, could be heard singing loudly and valiantly for a good part of his journey. It worked. Skiboo never caught him.'

Skiboo.

I also remember Skiboo. He roamed the streets of Belfast and left his image scrawled, in chalk, on walls or pavements above the words 'Skiboo wuz here'. He was more of a joke to children in Belfast than anything else and we drew Skiboo all over the place!

Jay continues, 'Petrol was strictly rationed, private cars were not allowed on the roads without special permission. Permitted vehicles, such as vans and lorries, or cars that had legitimate business purposes, had their headlights dimmed by a metal cover, which only permitted a thin slit of light to show. This was to conceal the whereabouts of vehicles from enemy eyes. We used to walk at night to church and school functions using dim torches. Cars had dim lights that were focused on the road.'

Blackout sometimes caused unexpected deaths, such as that found by **François Vincent** when he delved through old issues of *Banbridge Chronicle* and found that blackout in Banbridge town centre had tragic consequences for a 22-year-old soldier in late November 1941. The unfortunate gunner, whose ability to assess the height of the stone wall at The Cut was impaired by the prevailing darkness, jumped to his death – a sheer drop of 17ft.

The following report was published in the 6 December 1941 edition of the *Chronicle*:

The Cut in Banbridge was the scene of a fatal accident on Saturday night last when a soldier, Gunner Robert Dixon, aged 22 years, acting in ignorance of its construction, vaulted over the wall, and, falling a distance of 17 feet to the road below, was so severely injured that he died in the District Hospital on Monday morning.

The accident, which occurred in Newry Street, was investigated at an inquest conducted by Mr. R. S. Heron, Coroner, on Monday.

Although deceased did not answer any questions, when he was being dressed she (witness) heard him saying that he thought the wall was the same height on both sides and that he seemed to be falling miles.

Witness interviewed Gunners Gray and Shaw, and Lance Bombardier Smyth, who had been in company with Dixon.

He was informed that they had all suggested vaulting the wall and that Dixon had vaulted first; also that they heard him screaming on the other side.

They added that they had only been a few weeks in the district, and they thought the wall on the other side was the same depth as they were standing.

Banbridge site of fatal accident. (Sourced by François Vincent from *Banbridge Chronicle* archives)

From the top of the wall to where Dixon dropped was 17 feet, and the wall was three feet high where they were standing in Newry Street.

This concluded the evidence, and the Coroner returned a verdict that the cause of death was shock, following extensive bodily injury sustained by an accidental fall when he vaulted over the wall in Newry Street, in the blackout, not knowing the nature of the street.

The ARP (Air Raid Precautions)

When war was declared, my father joined the ARP. I thought he looked marvellous dressed in his uniform, a navy blue boiler suit and a tin helmet. After his first meeting he came home and annoyed my mother by sticking strong transparent tape in a tight lattice pattern all over our windows. She said she couldn't clean the windows with that stuff stuck all over it. Dad insisted, 'We need that tape. If you can't clean the windows they'll just have to stay dirty until the war's over. That tape could save your life. If the glass is broken in an explosion the tape will keep it from flying all over the place and cutting you to pieces.' She was horrified at the idea of having dirty windows. What would the neighbours think? Dad assured her that everyone would be in the same boat, so she needn't worry. In those days one was very conscious of what the neighbours might think!

Dad said, 'If there's an air raid what would you rather have, dirty windows, or death by flying glass? I'll have to go out and do my bit. The safest place for you to go is under the stairs. Staircases are much stronger than ceilings.'

My informants who lived in rural areas have told me they did not have sticky tape on their windows.

Air Raid Shelters

Belfast, the city with the highest population density per area in Britain at the time, also had the lowest proportion of public air raid shelters. Prior to the 'Belfast Blitz' there were only 200 public shelters in the city. They were disastrous because the basic brick side walls were not reinforced (see Chapter 5, 'The Blitz', with reference to Percy Street). They did have a solid, reinforced concrete roof. That was fine if a bomb landed on top of the shelter, but if it landed beside one the explosion caused the sides to collapse and the heavy concrete roof fell on top of the occupants and killed them. Bad as they were regarding protection, they were stronger than the local mill houses (see Chapter 5).

Air raid shelter in grounds of Dunbarton House, Gilford. (Printed with kind permission of Beryl Higgins)

Around 4,000 households built their own private shelters in their gardens. These private air raid shelters, Anderson shelters, were constructed of sheets of corrugated galvanised iron covered in earth. Since most casualties were caused by falling masonry rather than by blast, they provided effective shelter for those who had them, although they were damp, smelly and unpleasant.

Auntie Sally's husband, **Don Anderson**, worked in the Castlereagh electricity sub-station near the junction of the Glen Road, and was deemed an essential worker, so the Electricity Board insisted on building him an Anderson shelter in his back garden. The Anderson family lived in Trigo Parade on the Castlereagh Road. Uncle Don didn't want a shelter; he said he'd rather be under the stairs with the rest of his family. He was told he had to use it. There was some sort of penalty if he was killed by a bomb falling on his house – I suspect, but don't know for sure, that his pension would have been forfeited. As a result, whenever there was an air raid the family sheltered under the stairs while he took a thermos flask and several rugs down to his shelter. He said, 'I felt scared sitting out there, in the dark, with the door shut. I could hear all sorts of bangs and explosions but didn't know if the house had been hit so I opened the door and watched. It was like a great firework display and I wasn't as worried because I could see the house. I knew it hadn't been hit. The noise must have frightened a rat. It came and stood in the doorway and looked at me. It was there for quite a long time, so I talked to it.'

Sandbags

Sand was very useful during the Blitz. It was put into bags and used to protect buildings by being stacked against them, and it was poured on top of the fires caused by incendiary bombs. Sand was dredged out of Lough Neagh with unexpected consequences. According to **Jay**, you could be happily paddling along the shore and suddenly find yourself in very deep water. She remembered after the war a little girl getting into trouble while paddling. Suddenly she was in very deep water and she began to drown. Fortunately a man was driving along the road beside the lough. He saw the child going down, jumped out of his car, dived in fully dressed and rescued her. Jay also recalls horses walking along the shore and suddenly they were swimming!

Searchlights

Belfast was practically undefended during the first Blitz on 7–8 April 1941. No searchlights were installed until 10 April. There was no smokescreen ability, however there were some barrage balloons positioned strategically for protection. Given Belfast's geographic position, it was considered to be at the fringe of the operational range of German bombers and hence there was no provision for night-fighter aerial cover. Indeed, on the night of the first raid, no Royal Air Force (RAF) aircraft took to the air to intercept German planes. On the ground, there were only twenty-two anti-aircraft guns positioned around the city, six light and sixteen heavy, and on the first night only seven of these were manned and operational.

George Wilson recalls the installation of a searchlight on Shane Hill Rock near Portadown. 'During the war soldiers came up our road to Shane Hill Rock, the highest point in the area at 332ft above sea level. (During the 1960s the landscape was changed as a reservoir was built there to supply water to Newry and Dungannon.) The soldiers built a searchlight there to send a bright beam across the valley, light up the sky and spot enemy planes. I was frightened. I lay in bed and trembled because I thought the Germans might drop bombs on my house! When I was older I discovered the search-light was to send a warning if enemy planes decided to bomb the big linen factories along the River Bann. Linen was used on the tails of Spitfires and Lancaster bombers because if they were hit by enemy fire the linen tore but was not as badly damaged as metal would have been.'

Water Tanks

Garnet Chambers says, 'I can remember big water tanks, one in Newry Street and one in Bridge Street. I presume they held water to help put fires out if there had been an air raid or fire of some other kind. There was a fire brigade in the town but this might have been a standby.'

A water tank was built in Orby Parade near my house (No. 5) but on the opposite side of the street. Our parents didn't pay much attention to it but we children loved it. It was a large circular structure with metal walls about 4ft in height. In those days there was no such thing as Health and Safety, so we were free to perch on top of the walls and use a net to fish in the water.

All kind of things are found there and we were particularly pleased if we caught a stickleback, especially one with a red breast. The poor things were then confined to life in a jam jar. We were very careful not to fall into the water because that would have resulted in a good hammering for getting our clothes wet. It never seemed to strike anyone that we could have drowned!

Gas Masks

It's difficult today to realise how frightened people were during the Second World War because they didn't know what was going to happen next. Fear of a poison gas attack led to the distribution of gas masks, which occurred, in England, in 1939.

Northern Ireland appears to have been slow in giving gas masks to the population. **Marianne Nelson** lived and went to school in Belfast. She recalls, 'In 1941 the government worried in case the Germans used poisoned gas as a war weapon, so everyone was issued with a gas mask. I was 4 years of age and at Everton Primary School. Every week we lined up for gas mask drill. We marched out of school, lined up in the playground and put our gas masks on. Gas masks came in little boxes and we had to carry them with us wherever we went.'

George Wilson, who lived and went to school in County Armagh, says, 'I was about 4 years of age when I was given my gas mask in the playground of my school, Ballydugan Primary School.' **George McBride** was given one when attending Longstone Street Public Elementary School (known as 'the Penny Bap'), Lisburn. **Jay** doesn't remember being given a gas mask because she was only a baby.

A recent photograph of George Wilson. (Printed with kind permission of *Banbridge Chronicle*)

She does remember seeing it sitting, along with those belonging to other members of her family, on a pantry shelf. It was a large one that held the baby, tied securely round the waist, safely inside. It had a large 'window' the baby could see through.

I remember a woman calling at our house and supplying us with gas masks. Mum was fitted with an adult one. I don't think my father was there. Perhaps he got one through the ARP. I thought it looked weird. She showed Mum how to place my baby sister in her gas mask (she had one like Jay's). I thought it looked cosy. After that it was my turn. She produced a gas mask with a face like Mickey Mouse. She and Mummy explained that it was fun and I would have it pulled over by head so I could look out and pretend I was Mickey Mouse. I thought that was a stupid idea but I didn't say anything. Mum was shown how to fit it. She did her best but my hair got caught up in the strap. It hurt and I screamed. The woman said, crossly, 'Here let me,' roughly grabbed the hold of me, pulled my hair, twisted my neck and nearly yanked my head off. It was a terrifying painful experience. I not only screamed blue murder, I struggled. When eventually she got it on, I panicked because I felt I couldn't breathe. The woman said, 'Practise putting that on every week. You might need it.' I was terrified and sat on the floor sobbing. Mum came back and scolded, saying she was ashamed of me carrying on like that!

My mother was very conscientious. She respected authority, so the following week she placed my wee sister in her gas mask, tried her own on and

looked round for me. I was hiding in the darkest corner under the stairs. She lifted me out. I screamed blue murder. She smacked me because I was crying 'for nothing', so I now had something to cry about! That was a common reaction at the time. My husband remembers his mother lining him and his brothers up before they went visiting, smacking each one in turn and saying, 'That's a warning! That's nothing to what you'll get if you misbehave when we're out!' Needless to say, they behaved like angels!

Old Granny, Martha Henry. (Photograph by Bill Henry)

I was saved from the terrors of my gas mask by old granny **Martha Henry**. Thank God she appeared in the nick of time, or I might have been scarred for life! Mum was struggling to get me into my gas mask and yelling at me to be sensible. I was screaming and fighting. Old granny saw what was going on. Mum explained she was told to practise putting on gas masks every week. Old granny said, 'Anne dear, that's a lot of nonsense! You'll have the child traumatised! There probably won't ever be a gas attack and if there is, Doreen's a reasonable wee soul. Explain that you know the mask is awful but she must put it on to keep the nasty Germans from making her very sore all over.' That settled it. The masks were stored under the stairs and never used.

Collection of Metal to Make Munitions

Pat McGuigan recalls, 'There was a shortage of armament stocks at the start of the Second World War, so the government requisitioned iron and metal objects to be made into munitions. Soldiers were commissioned to gather metals that would help the war effort and as a result wrought-iron fences and so on were removed from private and public properties.

A church bell, known as the Urney Bell, which measured more than 8 ft in circumference, hung in the grounds of St Mary's Church, Melmount, Strabane. The local parishioners didn't want to lose it, so they removed it and buried it in a secret location in the local parish cemetery. There it remained, buried and forgotten for so long no one could remember where it had been hidden. Eventually the new curate in Melmount, Rev. Fr John Convery, began a search and discovered it in a grave marked 'A. Bell' and it was resurrected!

In 1970 a new church of St Mary's was built. Rev. Fr. Anthony Mulvey was appointed P.P. Melmount in 1978. Several years later he had a plinth constructed outside the church and the bell was erected.

Effects of the War on Education

(see Chapter 1)

At the beginning of the war schools suffered little disruption because the devolved government didn't have a scheme to evacuate women and children. Many schools took matters into their own hands. By December 1940 Campbell College evacuated many of its pupils to Portrush. A number of its buildings were requisitioned by the War Office as a military hospital. Several other schools, such as Ashleigh, Victoria College and Richmond Lodge, established branches for evacuated pupils.

There was a shortage of teachers as many had joined the armed forces. Schools throughout the North suffered the effects of the Blitz because so many people became refugees, causing numbers of children in rural schools to increase dramatically while those in Belfast shrunk.

5

The Blitz

The Belfast Blitz consisted of four German air raids on strategic targets in the city in April and May 1941, causing high casualties. The first was on the night of 7–8 April 1941, a small attack that took place to test Belfast's defences. The next took place on Easter Tuesday, 15 April 1941. Two hundred bombers of the Luftwaffe attacked military and manufacturing targets in the city of Belfast. Some 900 people died as a result of the bombing and 1,500 were injured. High-explosive bombs predominated in this raid. Apart from those on London, this was the greatest loss of life in any night raid during the Blitz.

The third raid on Belfast took place over the evening and morning of 4–5 May 1941; 150 were killed. Incendiary bombs predominated in this raid. The fourth and final Belfast raid took place on the following night, 5–6 May. In total more than 1,300 houses were demolished, some 5,000 badly damaged and nearly 30,000 slightly damaged, while 20,000 required 'first aid repairs'.

My earliest war memory is when my mummy did a very strange thing. She lifted me out of my cot while it was still dark. I had a dirty nappy. She always noticed my nappy and said, 'What a dirty mess,' and made me comfy by changing it. This time she didn't bother. She rushed to the cubbyhole under the stairs and put me on the floor on a funny bed made of pillows and eiderdowns. Daddy put on his funny ARP hat and told Mummy not to worry. Nobody thought German bombers could fly as far as Belfast. This was probably another false alarm. The war wouldn't touch us but we'd better stay under the stairs as a precaution. We'd be safer there.

The whole world sounded as if it had gone mad. A loud wailing noise went on and on. Mummy said the noise was caused by sirens and I shouldn't worry about them. I wondered what war meant and what were German bombers? I fell asleep. (When I was born Old Granny had advised my parents to make sure I was used to plenty of noise, then I would be able to sleep through it. I still can!) I wakened up next morning in my own wee cot and wondered how I'd got there!

In retrospect I think this must have happened on 13 September 1940, when a lone Luftwaffe aeroplane strafed a trawler off Ballywalter and attacked a fleet of approximately fifty cargo ships and destroyers in Belfast Harbour. It was repelled by defensive fire, flew low over Bangor and dropped twenty incendiaries on the forecourt of Bangor Railway Station.

Next day Mummy took me round to Aunty Sally and Mrs Mac came in. I liked her. She was fat and cuddly with big boobs, a big smile, interesting looking flat shiny things in her hair, a pair of slippers with fur round the ankles and a flowery apron. She was very cross. 'Them ones up at Stormont is a pack of edjiots,' she said. 'They're doddering auld fools without an ounce of sense between them. They think them German bombers can't fly as far as Belfast, so they do. Stuff and nonsense. Them Germans ain't no fools, so they ain't. They know we've got the biggest shipbuilding yard in the world, an aircraft factory, all kinds of engineering, and a huge rope works. We produce linen and food. Them Germans is bound til want to give us a bloody nose. They'll make aircraft that can come here, so they will, and we'll be sitting ducks.'

Mrs Mac was right. The Germans bombed Belfast on 7–8 April 1941. The government had ignored all the warnings, in much the same way that present governments are ignoring scientific research on global warming. Everybody had become tired of false alarms and had begun to either ignore or feel excited by them. Daddy complained people laughed at him whenever he mentioned he was in the ARP and he said he was fed up learning how to do first aid, deal with stretcher patients and put out fire bombs.

According to **Brian Barton** in his book *The Belfast Blitz*, Belfast received fifty red alerts between 25 October 1940 and the first actual raid on 7–8 April 1941. Our defences didn't see the German planes flying over Belfast Lough on 18 October 1940. They took excellent photographs, which were discovered after the Germans surrendered on 7 May 1945.

Lone enemy planes laid mines in Belfast Lough, causing the harbour to be closed at one point, minesweepers to be deployed and the lough to be protected by barrage balloons.

Sirens sounded for the first time when a single aircraft flew over Belfast Lough and dropped a mine on Bangor on 25 October 1940. Belfast had no searchlights, no night fighters, no smoke screen and no observer corps. The mortuary could only hold 200 bodies and the city could only accommodate 10,000 homeless people.

I have vivid memories of the first 'proper' air raid on Belfast during the night of 7–8 April 1941.

Eglington Street in the docks area, Belfast, 1941. (Printed with kind permission of Brownlow House Museum)

Mummy lifted me out of my cot, took me downstairs, put me in the cubbyhole under the stairs and told me to stay there. I peeped out the door. Daddy was dressed in his ARP uniform. The noise of explosions and aeroplane engines overhead was deafening and our dog, Toby, was under the stairs howling his head off. Mummy went over to Daddy, gave him a big hug and said, 'I wonder if we'll see each other again.'

He said, 'I hope so,' kissed her, opened the front door and as he went out I saw the sky was red, lit up by all sorts of flashes. Mummy was crying when she crawled in beside me. I'd never seen my Mummy cry. I gave her a big hug and told her not to worry because, 'My Daddy would chase the naughty noises away.' She took me in her arms, stopped crying and cuddled me. I felt safe and went to sleep.

That became known as 'the wee raid'. It was a small attack that hit the area around the docks. There were only eight bombers over Belfast at any one time and the raid was probably used by the Germans to test Belfast's defences. Thirteen people were killed, twelve in the docks area, and some houses were destroyed. High explosives fell in the Newtownards Road, Templemore Avenue and Albertbridge Road district. A more vivid impression was left by about 800 incendiaries that fell on that part of the city. Most fell on empty streets and were put out quickly. There were devastating fires around the docks because a lot of highly inflammable material had been stored there, such as timber tar and grain. Later some timber was kept on the Stormont estate, the rest being taken by special trains and stored in fields near the railway stations in Banbridge and Castlewellan, while grain was stored elsewhere.

That raid put the wind up the government because it seemed certain that the Luftwaffe would return. There was no way I could sleep through the second air raid. I was terrified, but that's another story. It also put the wind up **Jim Doherty**, who was in ARP POST 381 situated in the dock area. While on duty he found nothing worked! He was supposed to phone for assistance from the ambulance service and/or the fire brigade, but the phones didn't work. The fire brigade were slow answering the calling but by the time they arrived the fire had got a hold and the water mains had been destroyed, so they couldn't do much anyway. ARP personnel had to run round on foot, or cycle, to get help for people who were injured or to put fires out. Roads in the area became impassable, water, gas and electric mains were disrupted and that was only the wee raid!

Belfast Zoo wasn't harmed but authorities felt if it did suffer an attack dangerous animals could escape and attack members of the public. As a result, thirty-three animals including racoons, a black bear, a hyena, a tiger, a lynx, six wolves, a puma, two polar bears and a vulture where shot. Several elephants were lucky. The authorities decided they weren't dangerous, so they survived and Sheila, the baby Asian elephant, was particularly lucky because her keeper, **Denise Austin**, loved her and took her home every night.

I used to love going to Belfast Zoo when I was a toddler. In retrospect, and unlike today (Belfast Zoo has become a major conservation zoo), it was a miserable place, as were all others zoos at the time. Sad-looking animals prowled up and down inside tiny cages and stared belligerently out at members of the public, and I thought they were wonderful. I loved going into the monkey house and was thrilled and horrified to hear all the children laugh and shout, as they do today, 'Look at the monkey's bum!' (I wasn't allowed to say 'bum'. My mummy said it was a rude word!) When I heard that the dangerous animals were shot, on 19 April 1941, I cried. Today I think the animals were probably glad to be put out of their misery but at the time I was very upset. I was delighted to learn the elephants had survived.

Before the war being a zookeeper was not an option for women, but here were so many men away fighting in the war that women were allowed to fill vacancies caused by their absence, and Denise Austin became the zoo's first woman keeper. She lived in 278 Whitewell Road, a typical small semi-detached house. She had a small garden and a garage, and it was one of the last places you'd think of housing an elephant! Denise's relatives had a farm and they gave her bales of hay to feed Sheila, so the baby elephant was much better off with Denise than it would have been in the zoo.

The Whitewell Road is near the zoo. It curves from the Antrim Road down to the Shore Road. Denise waited each day until the zoo was closed and quietly let Sheila out of her enclosure and led her down the road to her house. Local residents were very supportive and talked to them. They stopped at a shop, Thrones Stores, and the owner gave them stale bread. Sheila was naughty. She used to help herself to cabbages and other goodies that were on display outside.

I heard my father telling my mother the following story. I've no idea if it's true or not, but feel it's the kind of tale you couldn't make up! Apparently an old woman, who'd never seen an elephant, went into the local police station

Denise Austin and her mother with Sheila, the baby elephant. (Printed with kind permission of Belfast Zoo)

Sheila being greeted by a passer-by on Whitewell Road. (Printed with kind permission of Belfast Zoo)

and said, 'I saw the strangest animal outside the Thrones Stores. It had a tail at both ends. It was stealing cabbages with one of its tails and if I told you what it was doing with them you'd never believe me!'

My brother-in-law, **Alan Finlay**, was born in 1940. He was the son of **Major James St Clair Finlay** and his wife **Molly**. Major Finlay was away fighting in the war so Molly's sister, **Joan Hamilton**, came to live with her on the Whitewell Road. Alan says Molly and Joan remembered Sheila walking down the road with Denise.

Alan was a very contented baby and, on the day the animals were being shot, she heard him gurgling in his room. It was lunchtime, so she went to pick him up and discovered there was a monkey in his cot! He wasn't in the least bit disturbed. They appeared to be enjoying each other's company! The monkey must have climbed up the drainpipe and in through the open window. Molly was one of the few people to have a phone, so she phoned the zoo and a keeper came and collected it. It's a family joke that the wrong monkey was given back!

Monkeys and elephants weren't the only things walking round Belfast's Streets in the Second World War. There was a ferocious bad-tempered man, called **Buck Alec**, who had a pet lion he put on a lead, like a dog, and took on walks around the York Street area.

Buck Alec and his lion. (Sourced by François Vincent from *Banbridge Chronicle* archives)

I remember going shopping with Mum. We took the bus into the city centre, got off in High Street and walked up Skipper Street to the large Co-op in York Street, which was on the site of what is now the University of Ulster. A large man strode towards us with what I thought at first was a peculiar-looking dog. Closer inspection showed it was a thin, miserable-looking, mangy lion. Skipper Street was very narrow. Mum and I moved back against the wall until he passed. I thought I'd dreamt the whole incident until, years later, I read **James Galway**'s autobiography. He records that locals were more frightened of Buck Alec than they were of the lion because if 'yer man had a skinful of liquor he knocked the stuffing out of any man he met on his way home from the pub'. As a result grown men used to hide in doorways if they saw him coming!

Buck Alec was born in Belfast. He was officially a great fighter who became bare knuckle champion of Ireland. He got into trouble with the law and fled to Chicago, where he became **Al Capone**'s right-hand man. Eventually he double-crossed someone and had to move back to Belfast. I suspect the authorities were too scared of him to shoot his lions! He kept several in his back yard.

We spent Easter 1941 camping in the Mournes and had a wonderful time. We sang all the way home in the car and arrived back tired but very happy.

The air raid siren went during what I thought was the middle of the night. According to Jim Doherty's book, it sounded at 10.45 p.m. I was happy to be taken out of my cot to 'hide' under the stairs with Mummy and howling dog Toby. I scolded him and told him stop making such a racket. Mummy and I cuddled, playing 'spoons' in the dark. We had a torch but switched it off so we

Wild camping in Mournes. (Photograph by Bill Henry)

didn't waste the battery. I was confident my daddy would chase the 'naughty noises' away until there was an almighty crash. The whole house shook. I screamed. Mummy held me tight. I put my hands against her face. Tears were running down it. She said, 'We're all right but the house must have been hit.' We shook with fear, sobbing, clinging to each other, listening to the deafening drone of aircraft engines and the whine of descending bombs.

The noise stopped. The silence was deafening. Mummy said, 'I wonder if that's it. I think I'll have a wee look to see if the house is still standing.' We stayed in the dark as she pushed the cubbyhole door. It opened! We peered out. Nothing but blackness! Mummy switched the torch on and flashed it round, turned back and whispered, 'I don't believe it. The hall's perfectly normal. Stay there and I'll have a quick look round.' She used the torch to have a quick peep into every room. 'The house hasn't been touched,' she said. 'Oh God! Pity those who have actually been bombed!'

We didn't sleep that night. We just held on to each other and prayed.

Daddy came home safely. He said the waterworks and North Belfast had been badly hit. We were worried about what had happened to

Auntie Carrie and Uncle Willie Husband.

Auntie Teenie and her family in Morpeth Street, and **Auntie Carrie** and **Uncle Willie**, who lived near the waterworks. We were relieved when Daddy told us my grandparents would be all right because they were outside the bombed areas.

Belfast is a small city, so every family was affected. As far as my relatives are concerned, we were finishing breakfast when Auntie Carrie and Uncle Willie appeared carrying their much-loved budgie, Mac, in its cage. They had walked the whole way from North Belfast because the roads were impassable. Auntie Carrie was in a terrible state. Their home had not suffered a direct hit but it was near the waterworks and was damaged by bomb blast. All the windows were broken and it had neither gas nor electricity. When the all-clear sounded she, Uncle Willie and their daughter, **Maureen**, had crawled out from the cubbyhole under the stairs and picked their way through broken glass and other debris. Maureen's fiancé, **George Cairns**, had left her home shortly before the raid started. Uncle Willie said, 'She spent the whole night sobbing, "God please keep my George safe. Please keep him safe." She didn't seem to care about us, or even herself. It was all "my George".' At that-point Auntie Carrie started to cry, 'My poor wee Maureen. My poor wee Maureen. She's gone to look for George!' Maureen was tall and plump. She towered over Auntie Carrie. By no means of imagination could she have been called 'wee'. That puzzled me. We agreed to look after the budgie while they looked for another house. Mac repaid our loving care and attention by being found in the bottom of its cage several days later!

Old grannie, **Martha Henry**, said she wasn't going to let Hitler put her out of her house, so the family didn't join the rush of Shankill Road residents up the road into the hills. She, her daughter **Teenie** and granddaughter **Betty** sheltered in the minute cubbyhole under the stairs. **Old Jim** crawled under the scullery table. A bomb exploded in Percy Street, killing people in

Wrecked car and wrecked houses, Hughenden Avenue, Cavehill Road, 1941. (Printed with kind permission of East Belfast Historical Society)

the shelter and shattering windows in Morpeth Street, including those in Teenie's house. It blew the door off the cubbyhole, which landed on Betty's tummy. She was badly bruised and in pain for weeks afterwards. Jim was badly shaken, but unhurt.

My second cousin, **Arthur Wallace**, had spent a lovely Easter holiday in Ballynure with our relatives. They returned to find their home had been so badly damaged it was unfit for habitation, so they returned to Ballynure.

Granda Finlay arrived mid-morning. He'd walked all the way from Ballysillan across the city and up the Castlereagh Road to see us. He was very relieved our street was untouched. He said Belfast was a mess, the roads were covered in bomb craters, transport couldn't get through, most of the shops on the north side of High Street had been blown out of existence and people seemed dazed. He laughed as he said, 'I had a chat with a fireman who was standing having a wee smoke beside his southern engine in Clifton Street. He came from the South. God bless the South. They sent their fire engines up to help last night. Anyway, the man told me he'd helped dig an old woman out of her house. It had collapsed on top of her. When he uncovered her and she heard his accent she said, "You're from Dublin, aren't you? Well, I knew I was being pushed through the earth, but I didn't realise I'd gone so far!"'

Granda didn't stay long because his sisters had arrived from Ballynure and insisted he and granny go and live with them.

Auntie Sally and the neighbours were cock-a-hoop, delighted because they thought the bombers had mistaken the waterworks for the shipyard! After the war we discovered Hitler bombed the waterworks because he thought being without water would make incendiary bombs more effective in future attacks. Surprisingly, he didn't realise Belfast's main water supply came from the Silent Valley in the Mourne Mountains!

Belfast's mortuary only had room for 200 bodies, so the Grove Baths were emptied and bodies laid out there to be identified. Another temporary morgue was set up in St George's Market. Bits of people who couldn't be identified were gathered up and placed in two mass graves. If they were found with rosaries they were thought to be Catholic and buried in Milltown Cemetery. Those thought to be Protestant were interred in the City Cemetery. The smell of putrefaction haunted the streets.

Local hospitals worked past capacity, particularly the Mater Hospital, which bore the brunt of the attack because streets around nearby Carlisle Circus were flattened. Thankfully the hospital itself was not hit, but staff were almost overcome emotionally and physically as the wards became packed. Makeshift beds were squeezed in, more and more casualties arrived and they were attended in packed corridors while the dead were laid out on sheets in the hall. The writer **Sam McAughtry** tore his Achilles tendon while putting out an incendiary bomb. He was admitted to the Mater Hospital and wrote, 'The grey dead were already being laid out on the floor of the hall. The worst were the still women with my mother's hair.' When Dad came back from his work in the ARP he was in tears.

Margaret Farnsworth lived on the Falls Road in North Belfast and remembers the night of the Easter Tuesday raid and what she refers to as 'The Flight of the Post Van'. She says, 'On the evening of the Easter Tuesday raid and I was playing with my friend next door to my house in Clondara Street when the air raid sirens sounded. A few moments later my mother called me. I ran home and my older brother **Neilly** grabbed me and pulled me towards his friend **Tony McPoland**'s post van. I remember I was bundled into the back of the van and before I knew it was crammed with all the other children of the street and we were flying up the Falls Road towards the countryside. It was pitch black and we were going at breakneck speed without any lights. My brother shouted, "Tony for God's sake turn on the

Front and back of Templemore Avenue Hospital. (Printed with kind permission of East Belfast Historical Society)

lights before you hit something!" He yelled, "Neilly what about the bloody blackout, we can't risk the Germans seeing our lights."

'It seemed an eternity before he pulled over on Hannahstown Hill, where he and my brother got out and opened the van's rear door. The other children and I got out and watched the flares of the few ack–ack guns shooting at the planes circling over Belfast, which was ablaze! From our elevated position on the side of Black Mountain we could see the docks and shipyard area glowing red with flames, and the noise of exploding bombs booming in the distance. It was terrifying.'

Eileen McCormick says, 'My father was a shoemaker, who had a shop on the Falls Road. After the first air raid he remained in Belfast. Luckily my granny had rented a house, 33 Tullymore Gardens, Donaghadee, for the Easter period. At that time Donaghadee was popular tourist centre and granny wanted us to have a holiday there. My mother moved there with all of us and the rental period for the house was extended indefinitely. It was a parlour house and we thought it was very grand! Father came to see us every Sunday, but stayed in Belfast during the week to keep his shop running.

'I remember my mother being very worried about him, especially when Belfast was hit for the second time and there was much relief when we got news that he was OK. We went to the Convent of Mercy for our schooling.'

The late **Margaret Greer**'s experiences were recorded by her son **Patrick Greer**, who reiterates, 'It was Easter Tuesday 1941. I was 16 years old and was living in Colligan Street with my parents and six older brothers. It was just after dusk when the air raid siren on the police barracks on the Springfield Road went off. After the previous raid the week before no one was taking any chances and there was a mass exodus of Belfast people leaving their homes and beginning walking up the Falls Road towards the countryside. I was with my mother and father, some of my brothers a little further in front of us.

'We walked about 2 miles up the road to Turf Lodge and sheltered in Dan Magill's Barn, sitting on the straw bales and looking out over the city. We could see the German planes flying low over the city delivering their deadly payload of incendiaries and bombs.

'My mother was out of her mind with worry as my brother **Jimmy** was a fire watcher in Bridge Street (we later learned that Bridge Street had taken heavy damage). Many prayers were said that night I can tell you.

'He was employed in a jeweller's shop in Bridge Street and was fire watching that night. When the sirens sounded an ARP warden knocked on the shop door and told him to go to the shelter. He said, "What about the shop?" The warden took him by the arm and said your life is more important than the shop, so he locked the shop door and went with the warden to the shelter.

'When the raid was over, he emerged from the shelter to find a pile of smoking rubble where the jewellers had once stood. Bridge Street was devastated that night.'

Patrick Greer says, 'My father recounted the story of his time as a fire watcher in High Street, Belfast. He was employed by McAlinden's Bookmakers and everyone employed in the shops in the area were obliged to take their turn at fire watching. It was his turn on 15 April 1941.

'His job was to extinguish any incendiaries that fell on to the rooftops of the shops below. He was issued with a bucket of water, access to a water tap and a couple of buckets of sand with which to extinguish any fires that broke out.

'That fateful night he was in the attic of Woolworths department store on the corner of Cornmarket when the German planes came over. He said they were flying so low that if he had a stone in his hand, he could have hit them.

He said that Belfast was unprotected apart from a few ack-ack guns stationed around the docks area. The front of the *Belfast Telegraph* offices was badly damaged and the Central Library still bears marks left by flak eighty years later. Belfast City Hall was badly damaged.'

Vernon Finlay writes, 'My father, **Norman Finlay**, was an employee at the Shorts Aircraft Factory in Belfast. He remembered coming back to work on fire watch. He told me employees had to get buckets of sand, and go around the factory extinguishing fires caused by incendiary bombs and flares. They burnt through the roof and fell on aircraft in the course of production. They put the fires out with sand from the buckets. It was a terrifying experience as you felt very vulnerable running around with bombs and flares falling around you.'

Jim Taylor writes, 'On 16 April 1941 my mum, **May Lyttle**, and her sister **Betty** were walking up Percy Street off the Shankill Road when the air raid sirens sounded. They ran into the shelter because they were frightened but they only stayed there a short while because their widowed mother was on her own in Conway Street and they were worried about her being frightened. Reluctantly they left the shelter and got home safely.

'Later they heard on the radio that the shelter had a direct hit about half an hour after they had left. A parachute mine fell on Percy Street about 15ft from the entrance of the shelter. The roofs of bomb shelters were made of reinforced concrete, a slab that was 30ft long and 1ft thick, so they were very strong, but

Belfast City Hall showing bomb damage. (Printed with kind permission of Brownlow House Museum)

the walls weren't reinforced. They were built out of ordinary brick. The shelters remained standing if they suffered a direct hit, but if a bomb landed near them the blast caused their walls to disintegrate and the shelter to collapse. As the outer walls crumbled the large concrete roof fell, crushing those inside. If my mother and aunt hadn't decided to leave what they thought of the safety of the Percy Street Shelter I could not have been born on 10 May 1945 at 165 Conway Street off the Shankill Road, Belfast, two days after Victory in Europe Day, so I feel I was lucky because I missed the war.'

Jim (Jimbo) Conway writes, 'Lurgan mourned when, during the Belfast Blitz, the Guy family – **Henry William** (father), **Mary** (mother) aged 50, **Mary**, 22, **Reginald**, 10, **Sydney**, 12 – originally from Lurgan, were found dead on 16 April 1941 under the collapsed roof of the air raid shelter in Percy Street.'

Marianne Nelson writes, 'My earliest memory in life is the night that Belfast was bombed. I was 3 years of age. We lived on the Upper Crumlin Road, about 3 miles as the crow flies from the Belfast waterworks, which, it was thought, the Germans mistook for the docks.

'I woke up in the late evening shouting down to Mum, "What's that big pumping noise?" It turned out that bombs were being dropped in the garden opposite our house. We lost practically every window. Mum got my brother, David, and me out of bed and spent the night under the stairs. In the morning we went up to the comparative safety of our local doctor's house. They were Mum and Dad's best friends.'

Vernon Finlay writes, 'I collected memories from my wife's aunt, the late **Miss Wilhelmina (Winnie) Thompson**, who was born in Carnan Street, Belfast, in September 1921 and lived there with her mother, father and sister all her life until eventually she had to go into a nursing home. Winnie died in October 2020.

'She said, "My uncle **Billy Wright**, my mummy's brother, was an upholsterer, married to my **Aunt Ruth**. They had a good, newly built house on the Oldpark Road. When the war came Uncle Billy joined the Army and my Aunt Ruth was there by herself when **Wilbert** was born. Aunt Ruth's house was badly damaged by the bombing. A large piece of masonry came through the roof and fell on Wilbert's cot. Thank God Wilbert wasn't there at the time. My mother took Aunt Ruth in, she gave her the back room that held the cot and the bed. Uncle Billy and Aunt Ruth had a lovely home with nice furniture. We took some of it in, Mrs Kidd next door took some and my Aunt Essie took some.

Lizzie Henry standing outside her home, 1 Glencairn Crescent, Ballygomartin. (Jim Lyle)

'"There were some air raid shelters near us in the street and we would see people, droves of them, walking up Matchett Street going to the fields up at Ballygomartin. We didn't bother, we just took a chance.

'"I remember seeing a plane and there was this thing hanging below it and that was the bomb that fell on one of the streets near Carlisle Circus. It was like a square box. The house fell like ninepins."'

Jim (Jimbo) Conway describes the fear experienced during the Blitz by his family, who lived in Lurgan. He writes, 'My mother recalled taking to the fields and hills as they watched Belfast burn during the bombing on Easter Tuesday, 15 April, when 180 German bombers attacked Belfast, seeing planes dodging around the searchlights over Belfast over 21 miles away from where she stood. This was the beginning of a sustained bombing campaign by the Luftwaffe on Ulster towns and cities second only to that experienced by London in the Blitz. The family had a Jewish refugee staying with them at the time. Mother was a good Catholic. She was frightened and recalled vigorously praying, "Jesus Mary & St Joseph protect us," with their Jewish lodger repeatedly chiming in, "and me too!"'

Garnet Chambers lived, and still lives, in Banbridge. He says, 'Reaction to the Blitz on Belfast is imprinted firmly on my memory. I was in bed and asleep when the Luftwaffe bombed Belfast and didn't know anything about it until the next day. We could see the Cave Hill above Belfast from our house. My mother and father talked about the glow of the fires in the city and the searchlights. My mother had a sister who lived on Belfast's Cregagh Road. There were few phones and she was very worried for three or four days until a letter came saying that her sister and family were safe.

'I remember the next day being out on the Newry Road when a fire engine came racing past with its a bell clanging loudly. I had never seen anything like that before. It was one of those that came across the border to help in Belfast. They had realised that the situation in the city was bad but some of them who stopped in Banbridge when coming back a few days later said that only when they came over the hill [Newry Road, also called the Yellow Hill] and for the first time saw the smoke and sky at 25 miles it was obvious that things were far worse than they could imagine.'

Joe Furphy writes, 'During the Second World War, I lived in a house called Novella, 61 Castlewellan Road, along with my parents **Jimmie and Eleanor (Nellie) Furphy**, my sibling Jim and, at times, my grandmothers.

'In 1939, we knew our country was at war with Germany and that England, particularly London, was being bombed, but we didn't take it seriously. The war seemed very far away and few people believed Northern Ireland could be bombed. It was a long way from Germany, aeroplanes were a comparatively new invention. We were safe, bombers couldn't reach us, or so we thought.

'At the beginning of the war my father joined the ARP (Air Raid Precautions) civil defence unit in Banbridge during what became known as the 'Phoney War'. Annoyingly, ARP folk were teased and told they were wasting their time learning first aid and how to put fires out. Some people said a lot of what they did was a waste of money – like the blackout, which needed men spending time wandering around at night making sure no chink of light showed when there were no aeroplanes in the skies to see it!

'When he was in the ARP, Dad was stationed at the top of Banbridge's Old Town Hall to fire watch. He could see for miles around and was mildly shocked when Belfast suffered what became known as the 'Wee Raid' during the night of 7–8 April 1941 when a maximum of eight planes bombed Belfast's docks area. He described how the sky was lit up by incendiary bombs, fires and magnesium flares. During that attack Hitler saw how badly Belfast was defended and prepared for a full-scale attack. Belfast was an industrial centre supplying ships, aeroplanes and weapons, and was crucial to the war effort.

'Dad was also on duty during the "Big Raid" on the night of Easter Tuesday, 15 April 1941 when the Germans killed nearly 900 Belfast people, injured 15,000 (600 of them seriously) and made 100,000 homeless. Bombs were also dropped on Bangor and Newtownards, where eleven soldiers were killed in an Army camp. I have often wondered why Dad never spoke about that night? He talked about everything else but not that night. He must have been very upset by it.

'My uncle, **George Sands**, had moved to Belfast. He did very well in the grocery business. At the time of the Blitz he was living in Deerpark Avenue near the Waterworks. He and Aunt May had three daughters, **Betty**, **Eleanor** and **Barbara**. His house was badly damaged by a boulder crashing through the roof and the family were made homeless.

'I was horrified when I saw Uncle George shortly after the Blitz because he'd been injured and had a huge bandage on his head. That was one of the families that found it impossible to remain together. My parents brought my cousin Eleanor to live with us. She was older than me, 11 years of age, and she attended Abercorn School. I loved having her with us and we became great friends, and indeed we are still in touch; now 92, she's in a care home in Antrim. Unfortunately my mother became ill and couldn't cope, so Eleanor went to live with my mother's sister, my Aunt **Annie Thomson**, at Doughery.

'I don't think people in Belfast realised how scared those living outside the city were during the Blitz. Many folk, including my relatives living in the high ground of Ballycross, could see the red glow in the sky caused by bombs falling on Belfast. It was rumoured that the Germans, if they had spare bombs, dropped them on isolated country farmhouses and so people used to take shelter under hedges, or hide by lying down flat in fields of oats.'

Sean McIlroy recounts, 'My aunt, **Teresa McArdle (née McIlroy)** was a most unlikely spy catcher. She grew up in the 1930s on a farm in Aughnacloy, Katesbridge, and remembered the bombing of Belfast in the early 1940s. She told me she used to babysit for Coburn family, who were well-known locally as seed merchants.

'**Mr and Mrs Coburn** had to go to Newcastle to a business event and stay overnight in the Slieve Donard Hotel. Given the recent air raids by German bombers over Belfast, they were concerned about the safety of their young children, who were left in the keeping of my aunt. Mr Coburn gave her specific instructions about what she should do if there was another night's bombing in Belfast. She was told it would be preceded by a siren sounding in Banbridge. She was to make sure the curtains remained tightly closed to prevent any escape of light from the house. She was to take the children to an air raid shelter the family had in the garden.

'Later that evening my aunt and the children were upstairs preparing to go to bed when the siren sounded! My aunt was young, had never been away from home and was in a potentially dangerous situation. She panicked! She thought the bombs were about to drop, so instead of heading for the air raid shelter in the garden she told the children to go under the beds and hide! She switched out the lights in case the Germans would discover their whereabouts.

'Eventually the siren stopped but my aunt was not taking any chances. She told the children to remain where they were and she would peep through the curtains and look out in what was the direction of Loughbrickland. She vividly remembered seeing some German planes flying over Banbridge, their cargo evidently having been dropped over the industrial areas and port of Belfast. As she watched the retreat of the German planes she noticed one veering off from the pack and flying over the Loughbrickland area. A man "fell out of a plane with something on his back". She said he was hanging "by strings on a big egg". My aunt had never seen a parachute and that was how she described the event to me all those decades later.

'The following morning the Coburn parents arrived home and were told about the previous night's events. They were shocked my aunt had failed to use the air raid shelter. She was asked to explain herself. She did so and told them she had seen a German plane veering off on its own and "a man falling out of it on a big egg". The story seemed incredible! Mr Coburn must have figured she was telling the truth because the next thing she knew detectives from Banbridge Barracks arrived and interviewed her about the night's events.

'My aunt told me that subsequently a police and army search was carried out in the Loughbrickland area and a German spy with tent and radio was discovered in a forested area in what I assume was Whyte's demesne.

'That was a very important discovery as there were linen factories all along the Lower River Bann. They were vital to the war effort because the thread-manufacturing factories stopped their normal production and began making navy, khaki and Air Force blue threads used in uniforms for the forces. Spitfire and Lancaster bombers had tails covered in linen. If the tail was hit by enemy fire the bullet passed straight through and didn't cause as much damage as would have been done by the buckling of metal. Miles Messenger airplanes were manufactured in Banbridge.

'An article published in the 6 January 1940 issue of the *Chronicle* stated: "It is interesting to learn that the automatic telephone system will be introduced at Banbridge Exchange at 1.30 p.m. on Thursday next." The main submarine cable came to Northern Ireland via Donaghadee and radiated out to Antrim, Newtownards, Lisburn, Coleraine, Newry and Banbridge.

If the telephone centre at Donaghadee had been destroyed, communication to Ireland would be disrupted and it would not have been possible to give warnings of air raids. If a German spy had realised there was an important telephone exchange in Banbridge and got his message back to his handlers, the town could have been bombed. If the Banbridge centre had been destroyed there would have been no way the district could have been warned of potential attacks.'

Bridgeen Rutherford lives in Londonderry and recounts, 'In Londonderry a single Luftwaffe bomber dropped two parachute mines, one of which landed harmlessly in a sandpit beside a house in Collon Terrace. The other mine landed on Messines Park, a housing development specifically for ex-servicemen. Four semi-detached houses were destroyed and fifteen people killed. The Germans planned to drop magnetic bomb/mines in the River Foyle, which would have stayed dormant on the seabed until a metal-hulled ship passed overhead. They would have caused havoc in what was a busy Allied shipping lane when they attached themselves to ships and exploded. Unfortunately for residents of Messines Park, one of the bombs was released at the wrong moment and the result was the worst incident in Derry/Londonderry's wartime history.

Memorial plaque.

'The local newspaper, the *Londonderry Sentinel*, reported the following the next day but the paper was banned from giving the name of the city in the report, or saying fifteen people had been killed. Available information is scarce due to censorship:

Yesterday morning, after a raid on a Northern Ireland town the previous night, when a number of people were killed and injured and some damage was done to residential property, a Union Jack floated bravely over the pile of debris, which is practically all that remains of four houses, two semi-detached dwellings, in an ex-Servicemen's colony on the outskirts of the town. Here a bomb dropped in the garden and three houses were completely flattened, while only the ruined gable ends of the fourth still stands. At the bottom of the crater, lying on the heap of rubble, was the couch of the suite. The wreckage of a piano was embedded in the side of the crate. There was a pile with all kinds of furniture, some of which escaped damage, buried in it. Several bodies, some dead and others fatally injured were dug out of the mass of debris. Another bomb dropped in open country. The Pennyburn Roman Catholic Church and Parochial House, which is just opposite where it fell, had many windows broken. A local eyewitness said the church was protected from a direct hit when the statue of St Patrick on the outside of the building 'shoved' the bomb away!

'A family living close to Messines Park in St Patrick's Terrace had a new baby girl in the February of 1941. They had just got her down to bed for the night when they heard the commotion. They got the baby and themselves to safety downstairs in the cubbyhole under the stairs when the bomb exploded in Messines. The father went upstairs to see if everything was all right and found the baby's cot was full of glass. If she hadn't been taken to safety she would have been injured or killed by the glass coming through the windows.'

An 80-year-old lady, **Mrs Gilfillan** who lived near Messines Park, refused to leave her bed, although the bomb shattered her windows, blew her hall door off and shattered plaster kept falling off the ceiling.

Mr Brown came to the scene to see if he could help. He heard a baby crying, dug in the debris and found it lying between its parents, who had been killed.

Bomb damage in Newtownards Road, Ballymacarrett, East Belfast. (Printed with kind permission of East Belfast Historical Society)

Several days after the Easter raid Auntie Sally appeared and suggested we go and look at the bomb damage around the Newtownards Road. It was no longer cordoned off. I was packed into my pushchair and off we went.

I'll never forget it. Grey people with grey faces on grey roads rescuing whatever they could from grey wrecked homes. Whole streets of houses sliced in two looking like untidy doll's houses with curved upper floors about to collapse. A man carried a ladder to what remained of his house, propped it against the upper floor near the gable wall, tested the bottom couple of rungs and climbed up. A small crowd formed. He was handed a walking stick and began hooking it on things in the room. He rescued a chair and a 'goes-under' (chamber pot). It caused a lot of laughter! Then he hooked the stick around a leg of the wardrobe and pulled. The wardrobe toppled and slid towards him. A woman screamed, 'Get down Sammy! Get down! I've lost enough without losing you!' She turned her back and covered her eyes. We held our breath. The house shook and settled. The wardrobe fell on its side and hung over the edge of the floor. Sammy pulled it further towards the opening. It slid further out. A group men lifted it down to ground level. Sammy climbed down, thanked them and said, 'That wardrobe cost good money. We'll need it when we get a new place. We'll all just have to get on with it.'

Small groups of people stood around gossiping. A lone man was standing in the middle of the road looking at a bomb crater. He wore a grey duncher (flat cloth cap). His face was grey, his clothes were grey. He was all grey. The whole street was grey. In retrospect I think everything was covered in dust. A woman came up to Auntie Sally and said, 'Do you see that poor man

Bomb damage, Belfast Rope Works, East Belfast. (Printed with kind permission of East Belfast Historical Society)

there?' She pointed at him. We looked at him. She said, 'He left his family to check on his mother who lives up the street. He came back to find his house had been flattened by a direct hit. That hole in the ground is all that's left. He had a wife and four kids. His wife was a lovely wee woman. Gone! All gone! They've been blown to bits, so he doesn't even have their bodies to bury. All he's got is his auld mother and she's a right auld targe!' (scold).

There were two more major raids on Belfast and I can't differentiate between them.

On 4–5 May, 204 bombers attacked the city and killed another 203 people, and the following night, twenty-two more died. Half of the city's housing was damaged during the course of all the raids and 100,000 people were made homeless. Some left the city never to return.

During the last two May raids I sat close to my mummy with our backs against the wall, her arm around me and my arms around my knees, and, although I was terrified I felt better because of Auntie Sally. She was laughing when she came into the house, saying she and Uncle Don had had a great night at a dinner held by the Electricity Board for its staff. Belfast's Lord Mayor, **Raymond Calvert**, had recited 'Ballad of William Bloat', which is full of the black humour Irish people love, especially those living in Belfast. It's an outrageous tale of a man who hated his wife, so he cut her throat. He felt very happy having got rid of her until he became scared of what the law would do to him, so:

> He took the sheet from the wife's coul' feet
> And twisted it into a rope
> And he hanged himself from the pantry shelf,
> 'Twas an easy end, let's hope.

> He went to Hell but his wife got well
> And she's still alive and sinning.
> For the razor blade was German made
> But the sheet was Belfast linen.

Auntie Sally told me the Germans could bomb and terrify us, but they couldn't win because we were from Belfast! After that I kept saying to myself, 'The razor blade was German made, but the sheet was Belfast linen.' It was a comfort.

I'm not sure when the last warning siren sounded, only that it was towards the end of the war in 1944 or 1945. I was out with friends, playing skipping games in the street. We looked at each other in consternation before running back into our houses, as we'd been trained to do. The noise was terrifying, sirens, plane engines and shooting. I went upstairs into Mummy's bedroom, stood in front of the bay window and gazed at the sky. I expected to be scolded. Everybody knew to keep away from windows during a raid. To my surprise Mummy came and stood behind me. We watched a small lone German plane fly over Belfast, hotly pursued by British planes. It was fatally wounded. Smoke belched out of its rear. It nose-dived. The pilot jumped out. His parachute opened and he drifted towards earth. He looked very vulnerable.

I burst into tears. Mummy hugged me and said, 'There! There! The danger's over. You're safe.'

'That man's somebody's daddy,' I sobbed. Mummy said that he intended to hurt us. I sobbed louder than ever, 'I don't care! He's somebody's daddy.'

I was amazed to find many children enjoyed the Blitz. Pat Quinn recorded in his book *Dear Little Town* that he enjoyed hearing the sirens and watching the lovely red sky when his mother pushed his pram out of Newry, where he lived, and into the nearby hills.

A family friend, the late Roy Leinster, who was born in 1935, told me he thought the Blitz 'was great'! He lived in South Belfast's Carmel Street, off the Ormeau Road, in the area known as 'the holy land' (all the streets have biblical names). Every night his mother used to prepare a picnic. When the sirens sounded, she lifted her knitting, the picnic and a football. Local families met in Ormeau Park, the adults sat under the trees, the women sat and got on with their knitting while the children played football! According to Roy, it was like a day out at the seaside with the interesting addition of all sorts of fireworks and a beautiful red sky. South Belfast was not touched by the Blitz.

Both men have told me they were horrified when they realised the significance of the Blitz years later and felt guilty because they'd enjoyed it while others suffered. I feel their parents were very brave, hiding their fear and keeping the children happy.

6

Refugees

George McBride recalls, 'In the wake of the air raids, many families evacuated to the perceived safety of the countryside. My family evacuated to the Causeway End Road outside Lisburn in County Antrim, where my paternal grandfather, **James McBride**, a Boer War veteran, had a small cottage with a corrugated iron roof. There were no amenities of any kind except a dry toilet about 50 yards away. Lighting was by candlelight. Water had to be carried from a well, about 100 yards away. The only source of power and heat was a metal stove, upon which all water was boiled and all cooking was done. Primitive by modern standards, but much appreciated at that time.

'I was enrolled in my first school, the Free Public Elementary School in Longstone Street, close to the centre of Lisburn town and locally known as "The Ha'penny Bap". Every day at break time we were given a mug of milk and a lump of fresh bread. It was around this time that I learned what a queue was. The first thing I learned there was how to wear a gas mask and what it implied. This must have been the beginnings of my understanding of what was actually happening out there in the wide world. Then there was the Collect Waste Paper for the War Effort project. Initially all pupils were given the "rank" of "private" and promoted according to the amount of waste paper gathered. I rose to the rank of "major".

George McBride and his elder brother, John. (Printed with kind permission of George McBride)

'Apart from our endeavours to help with the war effort we were diligently taught the 3Rs. I enjoyed learning to read, write, spellings, the times tables, avoirdupois weight, £-s-d (pounds, shillings and pence, the currency at the time) and so on. Homework was done initially by candlelight, but soon progressed to oil lamps. One day, probably late 1943, as I was walking home from school along the Causeway End Road, I saw an American aeroplane make an emergency landing in nearby fields. It was probably a supply plane. Within a short space of time the plane was surrounded by jeeps, dismantled and towed away.

'Outside of school I enjoyed living in the countryside, often helping out at nearby Wilson's farm. I joined First Ballymacash Wolf Cub Pack, where I began to learn about semaphore and how sailors in ships communicated with each other, but perhaps my most enduring experience during those dark days was meeting one of our neighbours, **Dixie Munn**. Dixie had very short arms with deformed hands yet he was a talented watercolour artist. Sometimes he held his paintbrush in his mouth. He seemed to me to specialise in painting landscapes, aeroplanes, especially Spitfires, and portraits of prize-winning racing pigeons. It was he who explained to me how important Spitfires were in aerial warfare and how homing pigeons were so important in carrying wartime messages. I became his "assistant", preparing his paper by pinning the sheets to a board and immersing them in a barrel of rain water. In retrospect, I often wonder how many of his paintings, the paper for which I prepared, still hang on clients' walls!'

George's younger brother **Noel McBride**, who was born in 1940, writes, 'I was very young at the time and can only recall few things, and then only vaguely. I have a memory of lying in a pram under the shade of a tree and hearing other children (presumably my brothers and cousins) playing nearby. I don't know how old I was but if I was lying in a pram that is a clue!

'We were evacuated to Lisburn to escape the bombing. This was probably after the raids of 1941. Ravenscroft Avenue, which is about 400 yards from Bloomfield Street as the crow (or, more properly, the Luftwaffe bomber) flies, was very badly damaged and I suspect that is what prompted the flight to Lisburn.

'I recall hearing that in the crush at the station my mum felt faint and dropped me, and I was caught in time by a man nearby. I have no recollection of this.

'We fled to a small cottage on the outskirts of Lisburn, which I believe was owned by my paternal grandparents. We shared it with my aunt **May McBride** and cousins. I'm not sure if my uncle **Jimmy McBride** (Dad's brother) stayed there but Dad travelled up and down to work (shipyard) each day. I don't know how many rooms there were or how we were spaced out but I doubt if there was much elbow room.

'The cottage was situated, I think, off the Causeway End Road. It was down a lane to the left going out of Lisburn. When I drive along that road I try to figure out where it was but everything is different from my mind's image – built up, roads changed, etc. I know that George and John went to school somewhere along that road in the town's direction.

'There was a neighbouring cottage further down the lane occupied by a **Mrs Neill** and her husband, **Johnny**. They were very friendly and good to us. I recall playing on their floor with a ragdoll, which I cherished!

'I remember we had an outside toilet (non-flush, naturally!) which had to be cleaned out with a shovel and the contents buried in a hole! I recall me Da doing this. I also remember an incident involving the removal of a branch from a tree. Dad had tied a rope round the branch, sawed through the branch, picked up the rope, pulled – and the rope broke and he fell on his ass! It caused much hilarity.

Marion Wilson with her mother, Betty, father the Rev. Dr Clements and her brother, David.
(Printed with kind permission of Marion Wilson (née Clements))

'When the war ended we came back to Bloomfield Street, which, during our absence, had been occupied by Aunt **Sadie Kerr** (Mum's sister) and her family. I recall travelling back in the cab of a coal lorry, our belongings in the back.'

Marianne Wilson recalls being a refugee. She says, 'After our house was damaged in the Blitz, Mum, David and I went to live with my aunt and uncle in the manse at Kells, County Antrim. Dad had to stay in Belfast as he was the minister of Ballysillan Presbyterian Church.

'After a while we then went to stay with another aunt and uncle in Cloughmills, County Antrim. We stayed there for quite a few months including my 4th birthday, in which I received a lovely baking set including the old-fashioned cream baking bowl that was complete with dimples. I was thrilled!

'One incident of this time in Cloughmills sticks out in my mind. I was rhyming at Mum to come up and say good night, after about the third time my uncle, who was quite a cross man, came up and gave me a smack, but next morning, I came downstairs in my dressing coat and up onto his knee, as usual, to listen to the eight o'clock news. After that, he and I were great pals. He thought, this wee girl has spunk!

'One day Aunt Bertha was out feeding the hens when I sneaked up and locked her in the hen house. She wasn't exactly pleased, although I let her out after a few minutes. About forty years later I was at party in Tandragee when a very distant cousin came up and asked, "Are you the cousin who locked Aunt Bertha in the hen house?"'

'Mum eventually got a bit frustrated spending time in the same kitchen as her older sister, so she packed our bags and we came back to Belfast. We did not sleep in the manse, but rented a bedroom in a cottage on the 7-mile straight on the way to Antrim, and went in and out each day on the bus. We felt safe there.'

Jay recounts, 'During the bombing of Belfast, many evacuees headed for the relative safety of the countryside. This brought severe culture shock to both the evacuees (who in our area were allocated accommodation so unappealing they mostly headed straight back to Belfast) and their hosts. Some, however, stayed with country families, including ours, and remained lifelong friends.'

George Nesbitt, a farmer who has lived all his life on a farm down Kiln Lane on the outskirts of Banbridge, says, 'Our home was a full house during the war. Besides my parents, **Mary-Jane and Robert Nesbitt,** there was me and my two sisters, **Sally** and **Mabel**. Hospitality was also extended to my **McCracken** cousin, his wife and two children, and to four women refugees who worked in the office at Walker's linen factory.'

Florence Chambers records, 'My parents, **Billy and Annie Dickson**, had spare rooms and so housed Belfast evacuees. The entire **Elliott family** from Springfield Road stayed for a time. They also looked after a nephew and niece and they went to my dad's school, Skeagh National Primary, where he was headmaster. My father had a severe heart problem, his school was about 3 miles from home and he was entitled to a fuel allowance to enable him to continue teaching. His school grew from thirty-five or so pupils to in excess of eighty. It must have been an extremely tight squeeze as it was a two-room school. Two teachers were expected to cope with all those children, although a temporary teacher was eventually sent to help with the numbers.'

Jewish Refugees

The Nazis murdered 6 million Jewish men, women, children and babies in ghettos, mass shootings and in concentration camps and their efficient extermination camps. They murdered Poles, Serbs, political prisoners, gay people, ethnic minorities, mentally and physically disabled people, Jehovah's witnesses, communists, trade unionists, social democrats, and those whose religious beliefs conflicted with their own ideology. More than 2,.77 million Poles died during the Nazi occupation of Poland. Auschwitz–Birkenau was the largest concentration camp. The Birkenau end of the complex housed the chambers. They could murder 20,000 people per day. Hitler's aim was to exterminate the Jewish race and turn surviving Poles into slaves serving the German nation. Recently on a tour round Auswitz–Birkenau' I was horrified when I saw display cases full of spectacles that had once been owned by Jews, thousands of shoes and mountains of human hair, used to stuff toys and sofas. Human skin was treated and turned into wallets and bones were used as fertiliser.

Gertrude Warmington, known as 'Gerti', was a Jewish refugee, who escaped to Northern Ireland just before the war. She spent the rest of her life in the North and was buried in the Quaker graveyard at Moyallon. She was born in Vienna on 10 April 1924 and died on 25 July 2015, the daughter of Jewish parents, **Leopold and Ernestine Kessler**. Leopold was a government official. They had a nice apartment, many friends and they were delighted when baby Fritz – Gerti's brother – arrived. Theirs was a happy, close family. The children started and enjoyed school. Life was good.

Leopold and Ernestine Kessler. (Printed with kind permission of Charles Warmington)

Gerti was 8 years of age when Hitler seized power, 1933, in neighbouring Germany. Gerti's family was spared for another five years, until the annexation of Austria by the Nazi regime on 10 April 1938 – the cruel irony being that it coincided with Gerti's 14th birthday.

The Jewish community was ostracised overnight, with Jewish children denied access to education, while Leopold lost his job and was sent to work in a pig-processing factory. The family's home was seized and they had to move to a Jewish ghetto.

The pogrom of November 1938 – commonly known as Kristallnacht, 'the night of broken glass' – was particularly brutal in Vienna. Members of the Nazi Party and various paramilitary organisations were joined by civilians to form mobs that torched most of the city's synagogues and small prayer houses. Jewish businesses were also vandalised and ransacked.

Leopold was terrified for his children. He registered them as Catholics in an attempt to protect them. Then he heard of **Sir Nicholas Winton**, a British banker born to German-Jewish parents who had established an organisation to rescue children at risk from Nazi Germany. He managed to rescue hundreds of children by train on the eve of the war, including Gerti and Fritz.

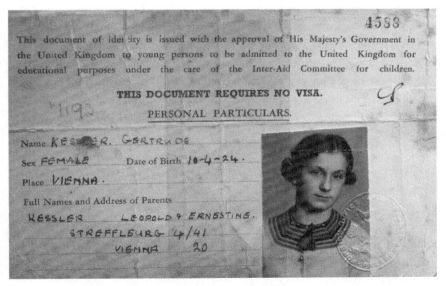

Gerti Kessler's identification paper. (Printed with kind permission of Charles Warmington)

As the train drew out of the station, Gerti's mother ran along the platform and shouted, 'Gerti, hold Fritz's hand tight and don't let it go.' Gerti held it tight for the whole journey.

Ernestine had given her children a small cardboard case with food for the journey, but they were so upset they couldn't eat it.

The train was constantly stopped by the Gestapo. Gerti and Fritz sat side by side, holding hands, not daring to look up as their papers were examined time and time again.

Having finally they made it to the coast, they didn't know where they were and they couldn't ask because German was the only language they spoke. Nobody came to meet them.

Eventually they were put on a boat and told they were going to London. They didn't know where London was! on arriving in London the children were again left standing alone on the platform of the station, until they were told they were going to Belfast. They had no idea where Belfast was! When they arrived in Belfast they stood alone until somebody told them they were going to Londonderry.

The British government had advertised for families who were willing to take in refugees – time was of the essence so there were no checks on those who volunteered. Unfortunately, Gerti and Fritz drew the short straw. An uncouth farmer picked them up at the station. He didn't want to care for traumatised children, he wanted slave labour. He gave the children straw to sleep on and housed them in his byre, along with the cows, and worked them hard.

After three days they ran away during the night and walked to Londonderry looking for help. Eventually they found a car sitting in the middle of a bridge with a man inside. Gerti knocked on its window and attempted a few words of tentative English.

The driver answered in perfect German! He was a German national who practised as a doctor in Northern Ireland. He took Gerti and Fritz back to Belfast. Heartbreakingly, the Jewish community didn't want to know them because they had been registered as Catholics.

The distraught siblings were then taken to Belfast Mission, run by the Methodist Church, and given a home at the Childhaven children's home in Millisle, in the Ards Peninsula.

Gerti spent wonderful years there. She and Fritz – renamed Fred – were able to resume their education at Millisle PS.

E̲ ʊ. märz 1941   *4*

Verzeichnis von Zahl IV/1o1-IV/199

1o1. LACHS Reisie Sara	22.11.1881
1o2. LACHS Anna false Ohlberg	1. 1.1906
1o3. LACHS Adele Sara	3o.11.1931
1o4. LACHS Biene	3o. 9.1904
1o5. LACHS Fred	27.11.1931
1o6. LAMBERG Laje Sara	18.11.1882
1o7. SCHIRMANN Maria Sara	19. 2.1893
1o8. MAHLER Friedrich Israel	25.11.1897
1o9. MAHLER Julius Israel	12. 8.1866
11o. MAHLER Sabine Sara	28. 6.1877
111. MARK Sara	24. 8.1888
112. CERNER Rosa Sara	8. 8.1873
113. KNEUCKER Alfred Israel	22. 2.1879
114. LÖW Frimid	15. 9.1888
115. DEUTSCH Ernestine Sara	14. 3.1871
116. DEUTSCH Gertrud Sara	26. 3.1901
117. LÖW Eugenie Sara	18. 6.1874
118. GROSS Fanny Sara	25. 9.1873
119. WELLISCH Irene Sara	2o.12.1893
12o. NEUNER Regine Sara	1. 8.1876
121. BALLA Blima Sara	3.12.1888
122. HAAS Arthur Israel	15. 9.1887
123. HAAS Beila Sara	12. 5.1886
124. SINGER Abraham David	7.12.1893
125. KOSS Malka Sara	18. 3.1895
126. KOSS Leo Israel	14.12.1927
127. KOSS Max Israel	1o. 1.1931
128. MISCHNAJEWSKA Gitl	1o . 3.1873
129. KESSLER Leopold Israel	2o. 7.1902
13o. KESSLER Ernestine Sara	26. 2.1902
131. GOLDSCHMIEDT Salomon	17. 7.1868
132. HELLER Chaim	24.12.1869
133. HELLER Fanny Sara	15.11.1878
134. FINK Salomon	6. 5.1877
135. FINK Cierel	5. 9.1874
136. HAUSER Gisela Sara	11. 5.1877
137. HAUSER Ernestine	24. 7.1900
138. HANDELSMANN Therese	11.1o.1886
139. THALHEIM Sofie Sara	13.1o.1878
14o. EISEN Kamilla	19.1o.1891
141. EISEN Harry	19. 1.1926

Record showing Leopold and Ernestine Kessler's enrolment in the concentration camp. (Printed with kind permission of Charles Warmington)

Eventually, Gerti trained as a nurse. As a first-year student she worked in what was then a TB hospital, Forster Green, in Belfast. The first time she was sent into the operating theatre she met the surgeon, **Dr William Theodore Warmington**, a young doctor and a Quaker. She fainted as he made the first cut! The pair fell in love and got married – people always said that Gerti had literally fallen for him at first sight.

Her brother Fritz/Fred moved to England and raised a family there.

Leopold and Ernestine Kessler were not as fortunate. They were deported on Transport Train 4 to Modliborzyce, Poland, on 5 March 1941. An archived list shows the deportees' numbers and dates of birth. Leopold is number 129. He is listed with the middle name 'Israel', which was allocated to all Jewish males. Ernestine's number is 130, and she was given 'Sara', the middle name given to all Jewish females. Leopold was moved at the end of September 1942 from Auschwitz to Zaklików and was then put on a mass transport train to Treblinka concentration camp, where he tragically died. Ernestine thankfully survived. She returned, with another former prisoner, from Poland to Vienna. They walked the whole way – a gruelling 450-mile journey.

After the war Fred managed to contact Ernestine and the family were united in his house in England.

Memorial plaque dedicated to Leopold and Ernestine Kessler. ((Printed with kind permission of Charles Warmington)

Gerti never forgot what **Sir Nicholas Winton** is reported to have said to the young refugees he rescued: 'Don't be content in your life just to do no wrong, be prepared every day to try and do some good.'

Gerti died in 2015 and was laid to rest beside her husband, who had predeceased her in 1981. Their diminutive resting place is marked by a discreet headstone, bearing both their names. It was placed horizontally, like all the other headstones in the cemetery, in keeping with the egalitarian ethos of the Quakers, a noble organisation in complete contrast with the ethnic hierarchy being promoted in such brutal fashion by the Nazi regime in 1938 – one that caused Gerti, her younger brother and others to flee for their lives in the first place.

Other Jewish children were housed at Ballyrolly House, also in Millisle, which operated as a refugee resettlement farm from 1938 to 1948. It is situated on the outskirts of the village and it became known as 'The Farm'.

Belfast's small Jewish community set up a refugee aid committee to raise funds from the communities of Belfast and Dublin, the Central British Fund, and later from the Northern Ireland ministry of agriculture. The Committee for German Refugees was launched under the umbrella of, and with funding from, the Joint Christian Churches, including Presbyterians, Methodists, Church of Ireland, Quakers and Catholics. They established a hostel in Cliftonpark Avenue, Belfast, initially adult refugees. Most Jewish, and some non-Jewish families, took a child into their home when the Kindertransport children began arriving and some members of the Refugee Aid Committee – **Barney Hurwitz**, **Leo Scop** and **Maurice Solomon** – leased a derelict farm of about 70 acres on the outskirts of Millisle, County Down, in May 1939.

The first children must have been horrified when they arrived from the Belfast hostel on a night of heavy rain and howling winds. They became soaked because their tents leaked. The next night they moved to a newly whitewashed cowshed and an old stable served as the dining room with rain trickling in. The latrines had to be dug.

Local people and the Belfast Committee helped clear fields. Adults and the older children dug, hoed and planted grain and vegetables, while the younger children gathered stones and uprooted weeds and thistles. Long wooden huts were built containing dormitories and some small bedrooms. Eventually, the cistern was cleaned and a rotary hand pump supplied showers, and flush toilets were installed. A recreation room, complete with

A recent photograph of a horse using the farm stable.

billiards and table tennis, offices and a small synagogue were built, and a large, twin-gabled structure containing a cow byre, work-shops and storage rooms. It's still in existence.

The farm was run like a kib-butz. All the children, even the youngest, worked on the farm, and were given a shilling per week pocket money, which later this rose to half a crown. **Eugen Patriasz**, a Hungarian refugee, was the farm manager and several local people were employed to teach the refugees farming skills and to work with them.

The farm became self-sufficient. In October 1940 its crops included oats, barley, wheat, carrots, onions, turnips, potatoes, Brussels sprouts, cabbages, cauliflowers and maize. There were seven cows, two Clydesdale horses and 2,000 chickens. In 1941 they bought a Ferguson tractor, helped by donations including one from the Dublin Jewish community and government grants. They had a workshop where farm and domestic machinery was repaired, and churned butter and cream in their dairy. They had a kosher kitchen, a laundry, a sewing room, a carpenter, and even a cobbler!

A Viennese saxophone player, **Erwin Yakobi** (known as Yakobi), was in charge of the children's health because he came from a medical family. He was a small, round man who managed, with the help of others, to weld young people, of different ages, from different countries and emotionally scarred into a thriving, working co-operative farm community.

The children went to the local, small two-teacher school, Millisle Public Elementary School. **John Palmer**, the headmaster, paired each refugee child with a local child to help them learn English. (The old school has been replaced by a modern building and has been renamed

Millisle Primary School. It has a modern sculpture inside the gates commemorating the Jewish refugees.) Lasting friendships were formed and the refugees were invited into local homes. When they were 14 years old many of the refugees continued their education at Bangor Grammar School, Bangor High School, or Regent House. Several went to night school in Donaghadee. They had the opportunity to join the local Scouts, attend Red Cross first aid classes, and the boys between the ages of 14 and 17 were able to join the local Air Training Corps.

The children played football with the locals, and had strong connections with Belfast's Jewish community. They loved the cinema and frequently walked the 3 miles to Donaghadee, where they were given free entry to the local Regal Cinema. Up to eighty individuals lived and worked on the farm at any one time from the first arrivals in 1938 to its closure in 1948. Well over 300 adults and children are believed to have passed through it.

Today the farm belongs to the **Magill** family. The present owner says it was bought by his grandfather in 1948. He has been asked if he's frightened working about the place in the dark as the traumatised Jews who took shelter there supposedly exist as ghosts. He says he's never felt that. He loves

Sculpture commemorating the memory of Jewish children's attendance at Millisle Public Elementary School.

Plaque at base of sculpture.

the atmosphere of the farm and I must say when I visited I loved the warm friendly feeling I got. He told me there was a cobbled path leading down the shore which the children used to use to run down to the beach to play, or to go swimming. Over the years people who lived in there during the war and/or their descendants have come back to visit and they all say that to them the farm was heaven.

7

Prisoners of War

Garnet Chambers records, 'As the Allied armies pushed into Europe, prisoners of war were taken in great numbers. There were many PoW camps in Northern Ireland and one of them was at Gilford. The field, now Beechlands, in Banbridge was put to use. A big field kitchen was erected along with other temporary buildings. The PoWs were brought from Gilford in lorries each day and put to work levelling where all the trenches and shooting range, etc., had been. I suppose that it was as much to keep them occupied as anything. Water had to be carried and to get it squads of four or five Germans with two buckets apiece went to a house along the road from us where there was a pump. Back and forth they went all day. Productivity would have been very low as even I, a small boy, could see that the buckets were only half full. Two soldiers wandered along behind them, sometimes with their rifles at the ready and sometimes with the rifles slung over their shoulders. Sometimes the guards coming behind the prisoners would have shaken their heads as they came near our house and we came to know that at least one PoW was to be watched very closely. As one soldier said to my mother and another woman, "That one there," indicating a tall blond one, "he's a right Nazi bastard." Fraternisation was strictly forbidden but if some of my cousins from Belfast were visiting us the soldiers would have stopped to chat them up. The Germans simply sat down on the grass and had a rest. I don't suppose that they were at that work more than a couple of months but I remember my father coming home one evening from work and saying that when he had been coming home for lunch that day they had been digging a large hole and when he was going back again another group were filling it in.

I think a deal of that went on. I speculated with my father if there would be Japanese prisoners coming but he said that it would be too far to bring them. I was a bit disappointed.'

There was a prisoner-of-war camp at the bottom of Ballymoney Hill, Banbridge. (The site is now occupied by a youth centre). They were confined by rolls of barbed wire. According to **Margaret Graham**, the German prisoners used to shout at passers-by, 'We will live to fight another day.' Margaret said, 'They were just young fellows and nobody paid much attention to them.'

My old friend, the late **Edith Chapman**, told me of the difficulties she experienced when working as a civil servant in Stormont. She was a teenager at the time and as the office junior she was often sent on an errand across to Stormont Castle. To do so she had to walk past an enclosure that housed German PoWs. When they saw her coming they used to rush to the fence 'like a crowd of wild animals' and shout filthy, sexist remarks at her. She didn't pay any attention to them but felt terribly embarrassed and was sure her face went as red as a beetroot. One day, when what she described as a 'wild wind' was blowing and she was wearing a full skirt she had difficulty controlling it along with the files she was carrying! Seventy years later she still blushed at the memory!

German prisoners of war in Curragh. (Sourced by François Vincent from *Banbridge Chronicle* archives)

German prisoners of war enjoying a night out in the Curragh. (Sourced by François Vincent from *Banbridge Chronicle* archives)

Those prisoner-of-war camps were very different from the one in the Curragh, near Naas in the South, and another one outside Gilford in County Down.

Once, while on a family smuggling trip south during the war (see Chapter 8) we were astonished, and furious, to see German soldiers sightseeing in Dublin on O'Connell Street. I remember thinking, 'They're the enemy. They bombed Belfast. We should do something about them!' I asked my daddy if we could kill them. He said, 'No! We can't do that. It's not possible. We don't have any weapons. We'd get caught and be sent to jail and we couldn't go home and eat those lovely Hafner's sausages and the delicious frying steak.' So I discarded all murderous ideas!

Years later I discovered the reason we saw German soldiers walking around in Dublin during the war. Ireland, as a neutral nation with negligible military power, went to great efforts to maintain that neutrality. It negotiated with both the German and the Allied governments and came to an arrangement whereby combatants, of any nationality, who accidentally arrived in their country would be interned.

One camp was set up in the Curragh, near Naas. It looked like a normal camp, with barbed wire, watch towers and so on, but it was far from normal. The fence separating British and German soldiers was only 4ft high. Prisoners could wear civilian clothes, although the Germans choose to don their uniforms. The guards had blank bullets in their rifles and prisoners were allowed to run their own bars with duty free alcohol! Prisoners could

British prisoners of war. (Sourced by François Vincent from *Banbridge Chronicle* archives)

borrow bicycles and leave the camp if they signed a parole paper at the guardhouse and gave their word of honour not to escape. There were evening dances in local dance halls, pub visits with separate bars for different nationalities, fishing and golfing trips and fox hunts. One English officer even had his horse transported from home, while others were joined by their families for the duration of the war. Some prisoners married local girls. Some, like Georg Fleischmann, a German, never went home. He stayed and became an important figure in the Irish film industry. There were few attempts to escape. The sea acted as a barrier.

A Canadian bomber flying from a base in Scotland got lost and crashed near what they thought was their airfield. They saw a pub and decided to have a quick drink to celebrate their survival. They were astonished to see a group of soldiers wearing Nazi uniforms and singing in German. When the Germans saw them they shouted, 'Go to your own bar.' The crew discovered they'd crashed in the Republic of Ireland and there were separate bars for Germans and the Allied forces. The Canadians were captured, just like the Germans, and had to suffer a comfortable war with plenty of distractions!

Roland Wolfe, known as Bud, was an American who lost his citizenship because he signed up with the RAF before the US entered the war. He was stationed in Eglinton and was flying cover for a ship convoy that left the safe harbour in Lough Foyle and headed across the Atlantic. On his flight home his Spitfire's engine overheated and he had to force land on a bog in Donegal in November 1941. He parachuted out safely and didn't know where he was. He thought he'd managed to come down on British soil and was horrified to find he'd landed in the South! He was picked up by the garda, taken to the Curragh prisoner of war camp and interned.

Bud didn't want to sit twiddling his thumbs, so he decided to escape and go back to his post. In December 1941 he signed out of the camp, walked out and 'forgot' his gloves. He returned for them and left again without signing a new parole paper, so he now considered his escape legal. He had lunch in a local hotel, made his way to Dublin and boarded the first train to Belfast before travelling back to Eglinton. To his surprise, his superiors were furious! They were very conscious that traditionally Ireland has been used as a back door to attack England, so they didn't want to jeopardise the South's neutral status. They sent Bud back across the border to the prison in the Curragh.

Bud eventually became involved with a 'proper' escape plan. He, along with other prisoners, secretly dug a tunnel out of the camp and escaped through it. He was caught and sent back so he gave up, made the best of it and joined the fox hunting with relish. His story didn't end with his death in 1994 because his Spitfire, along with 1,000 rounds of ammunition and six machine guns, was found by a team of archaeologists in June 2011 in the Donegal bog where it had crash landed. It was very well preserved thanks to the highly unusual, soft nature of the terrain and was the subject of a television programme by **Dan Snow**.

There was an equally strange prisoner-of-war camp outside Gilford, County Down.

The late **Joan Gafney** told me about it. The camp was on the left-hand side of the road when travelling on the road going from Gilford towards Lurgan, about halfway between Gilford and Ballydougan Pottery. The prisoners there were German nationalists who had been employed locally before the war. The government imprisoned them in case they were spies. The kindly Gilford people were sorry for them and, as the camp was in the middle of rich farming area, used to supply the prisoners with extra rations, such as butter, milk, cream, eggs and home produce, including delicious home-baked tarts and cakes. Each night the prison warders dutifully locked them in. There was a loose wire fence at the back of the prison, so the inmates could get out and visit local friends and pubs, where they often met and had a bit of craic, often with the warders who'd locked them up!

In the 1970s my husband, **George McBride**, became headmaster of what was then Craigavon (now Gilford) Primary School. Sometime later we went on a holiday to Lough Erne, where we met **Miss Grosse,** who taught German in my husband's old school, Grosvenor High School, Belfast. When she heard my husband worked in Gilford she laughed and said, 'I love Gilford!' We asked her how she'd come to know, and love, a small village in County Down. She said, 'I came over to Northern Ireland in the 1930s to improve my English. I loved it and never went back! I was locked up in Gilford, if you'd call it that, along with other German nationals, during the war. The local people were so good to us we couldn't believe it! We had the kind of experience you'd only get in Ireland. We were locked up every night, got out through a loose piece of wire in the back fence and went visiting. I think some of the local girls became pregnant. We loved being prisoners and loved Northern Ireland. When we were repatriated we cried our eyes out. We didn't want to go back to Germany and pleaded to be allowed to stay. The government insisted we had to return to our homeland. The first thing we did when we got there was buy a single ticket back to Northern Ireland and, as far as I know, we've all been here ever since!

8

Smuggling

The United Kingdom wasn't self-sufficient with regard to food production before, during and after the Second World War, so it had to be brought in from outside. Hitler believed if the country was starving, its inhabitants would become weakened and surrender. The Germans did their best to sink every vessel sailing in the Atlantic Ocean and the seas around the British Isles, so rationing was introduced to make sure nobody starved.

Petrol was the first thing to be rationed after the war began on 3 September 1939. On 8 January 1940, bacon, butter and sugar were rationed and families were issued with ration books. Meat, lard, tea, jam, biscuits, milk, tinned breakfast cereals, cheese, eggs and dried fruit were also subsequently rationed.

The late **Dolly Skuce** spent the first year of the war living in Cork, with her husband, **Sam**, a bank official. Sam was promoted early in 1941 and the family relocated to Belfast. Dolly writes in her book *Magic Lanterns to Moon Landings*, 'In the last few days we were in Cork rationing had been introduced half an ounce of tea per week! You should have heard the uproar, including my family. We would use that for our early morning tea!'

Cork, like the rest of the South, was interested in the war and war news, but Belfast was deeply involved. Rationing came as a shock and Dolly felt she had been thrown in at the deep end. She found obtaining ration books was a chore because she didn't know where to go and so on. Each family was entitled to:

2oz butter per person per week

2oz margarine per person per week

1oz lard (or cooking fat) per person per week

2 oz bacon (or rashers) per person per week

1 egg per person per month

1s 6d worth of meat per person per week (which bought 4–6 oz of meat, depending on the type purchased.)

A points system started when each person was given twenty points per person per twenty-eight days! They were used for 'luxury' items, such as a tin of salmon, dried fruit, or perhaps a tin of fruit. If you saw a queue, you joined it. You didn't know what you'd get when it was your turn, but you were glad to have it!

Food was cheap because the government kept the prices down. Frozen beef from Argentina was available for six months of the year and for the next six months we ate frozen lamb from New Zealand. My family preferred lamb from New Zealand to the Argentinian beef, but there was nothing to beat meat smuggled over the border from the South. It was a rare treat!

Northern Ireland is the only part of Britain that has a hard land border with another country. The Republic of Ireland was not in the war, had more goods and they were much cheaper than in the North, so smuggling became a national pastime during and after the war. The South was short of tea, which they smuggled along with bread. Northern bread was lighter in colour and tasted better than that available in the South. People caught smuggling received sympathy rather than condemnation.

Clothing was rationed between 1941 and 1949. Each autumn my sister and I were taken to a dressmakers' and a new coat and skirt was made for us, while Mum either bought, or knit, us a new jumper. We also had a new hat, gloves and shoes and socks. We wore our new outfit to church on Sunday and last year's clothes to school every day during the week. Our clothes were washed on Saturday while we wore our very old clothes. In the spring we were given a new dress, cardigan, short ankle socks and a pair of sandals. With so few clothes it was considered a major offence to get them dirty. We took advantage of my father's job. He worked in what was then the Ocean Insurance Company, in the Ocean Building on the corner of Donegal Square East and Chichester Street across the road from Belfast's City Hall. Throughout the war until 1950 he insured scutch mills. He travelled around the country inspecting mills and made sure they had all the recommended safety devices in place. As a result we were an unusual family because we had a car and Dad had a petrol allowance.

Very occasionally Dad drove over the border and, during school holidays, my sister, Eileen, Mother and I were taken along for the ride and left to our own devices while Dad did whatever he had to do. We might go to Dundalk and be dropped off and left to wander the streets. We salivated at the cheap goods while sucking a rare treat – sweets or ice cream. Once Mum bought us sandals and told us to scuff them up a bit so they didn't look new and wear them going home. I was surprised when the customs man put his head in the car window, said, 'Anything to declare?' and Dad replied with a firm 'No!' I'd been taught never to tell lies, and there was my father telling one fit to choke an elephant. My sister and I were wearing several sets of knickers and vests and our new sandals!

I loved the mixture of fear and excitement at the border. Mum said I looked as if butter wouldn't melt in my mouth, so when she bought big juicy steaks and Hafner's sausages she stuck them up my oxter (armpit) under my coat and told me to use my arm to press it tightly against my body. She asked me to sit forward so the customs could see I had nothing behind me and to smile at him. I think the smile might have been more of a grimace! Meat from the South was delicious, much better than the stuff we could get at home.

Doreen McBride (née Henry) dressed to go smuggling.

Once Mum dressed us in our old coats, which were too short and too tight. I thought we looked like scarecrows and was relieved when she took us into Clery's and bought us new ones. We felt very smart and very worried as we passed through the customs on the way home! As far as I remember we left the old coats in the Clery's ladies! Mum said she was sure somebody would put them to good use.

Dad said when he was alone the customs questioned him, had a quick look at the back seat and might open the boot. They rarely looked at the passenger's seat, so he started bringing parcels of meat over the border by putting them where a passenger's feet would be.

Once the customs asked Dad if he'd give an officer a lift. Dad said, 'I nearly had a hairy fit. I couldn't say "No" and I'd our meat sitting on the floor at the passenger's side. When yer man got in I said, "Please keep your feet off the contraband." He laughed, put it on the back seat and we'd a great bit of craic!'

In the late '50s Dad bumped into that revenue man again, who said he'd retired and told Dad about a lorry driver who used to go across the border every day with an empty lorry and return with an empty lorry. They knew he was smuggling something but couldn't fathom what, although they practically took the lorry apart searching. After he retired he saw the lorry driver in a pub and said, 'It's too late now to do anything. Would you mind satisfying my curiosity by telling me what you were smuggling?'

'Petrol! I had an extra big tank. I filled it up in the South, returned home and sold it. I made an absolute fortune.'

People who had the greatest chance of smuggling were those that lived on the border, such as Belcoo in the North. Walk down the street, cross the bridge over the river and you are in Blacklion in the South.

Bridie McGillian lives in Strabane, which is on the border. Walk across a bridge and you're in Lifford, a town in the South! Bridie says, 'My mother and I were good smugglers, living on the border as we did. We went regularly to a small shop lit with an oil lamp, and open until late. So a good wet night meant the custom officers didn't come out a lot. Rain capes were fashionable, so you wore one over your coat. We usually did well with sugar, butter, eggs and other groceries. During the holidays my friend and I smuggled door mats, wallpaper, dress and curtain material wrapped round us with the help of the shopkeeper and then a belt to keep it all secure.

'One day I was sent to get butter. I took my little sister, who was a toddler, in her buggy. I flattened the butter and put it behind her under her coat. On my way back a custom officer crossed the road to stop me. I was scared! He asked, "What are you doing over here? Did you buy anything?" I said, "Sweets," and when he asked where they where I said we'd eaten them.

'I'd been told if they found anything in a pram, they took it off you. I was shaking. I thought they might take the baby too. That was my worst trip and I was about 9 or 10 years old!

'On another occasion I was sent across to buy a small brown case my mother wanted. My dad was going away for a few days and needed it. He always went to an annual meeting of the Foresters (I.N.F.). I took some of my clothes and a pair of slippers and put them under my coat.

'When I got to the shop I bought the case and put the spare clothes in it and made my way to the station to get the train to Strabane, about half a mile away! I had walked over the border! When I got off at the end of my "long" journey I queued up with the other travellers and put the case on the trestle table, opened it and waited with baited breath while its contents were inspected. No bother! I closed it up and went home. Mission accomplished!'

Frankie Elliott also lived in Strabane and says, 'Smuggling was common. Many shopkeepers had a business on both sides of the Strabane–Lifford Border. White loaves and white flour were not available in Donegal, so they had to use a darker flour.

'Butter, meat, fags and tobacco and ladies' nylon stockings were much sought after. Local chemist shops sold "leg tan", which women used to paint their legs brown, then draw a seam up the back of them with an eyebrow pencil.

'Men who could afford it walked across the border to Lifford and bought a few bottles and a pound of Andy the butcher's mince. There are those who say that most of the stout bought walked back across the border in the men's stomachs. Sugar was scarce in Northern Ireland and plentiful in Donegal, so it formed a big part of smuggling, while tea went the other way.'

Noel McBride was born in Belfast and recounts, 'My parents used to go to Dublin on the train. I wore my school cap, which has a seam where the stitches had come out so we were able to stuff my cap with stockings and I came home with a bigger head than usual!'

Noel McBride with his parents, Martha (Cissie) and George. (Printed with kind permission of Noel McBride)

George Beattie was born before the Second World War in Euston Street, Greenore. He was the youngest of five children and in many ways he had the best of both worlds because he lived in the South and went to Newry Model School in the North. George says, 'There were forty houses in Greenore and we all got on very well. I think my regular trips to school were looked upon as an advantage because many neighbours had relatives, or friends, who lived in England and they wanted me to post parcels to them. Nobody knew the price of postage without going to the post office to have the parcel weighed, so my neighbours always gave me enough money to cover the cost, and any change was payment for the postman!

'My school friend, who lived in the North, had ration coupons for sweets, but no money. I had a certain roughness of money, left over from posting parcels, but no coupons because I lived in the South. We used his coupons and my cash to buy sweets and shared them.

'I travelled North by train. Trains were very different in those days. Each coach had seven individual carriages linked by a corridor. The carriages were great for smuggling! Goods could be hidden under the seats, the seat cushions were removable and if a pound of butter or a loaf was slightly flattened, it could be secreted behind a cushion, as could a parcel destined for England. If the customs men found goods, they were confiscated. In that case we all swore blind we knew nothing about it!

'Every week I smuggled a pound of butter North and gave it to my friend in exchange for a quarter pound of tea, which was in short supply in the South. There was a popular rhyme at the time:

God bless De Valera and Sean MacEntee
For the brown bread and half ounce of tea!

'Bread in the South was horrible. It was dark brown in colour and tasted awful, so every day I brought a couple of Northern white loaves home.

'Having a friend in the North was very useful because two of my brothers and my sister served in the British armed forces. They didn't dare come home wearing their British uniforms because they'd have been arrested and sent to the prisoner-of-war camp at the Curragh (see Chapter 7) because the North was a foreign country. They kept their uniforms in a friend's house in Newry, went there and changed into their civilian clothes. They reversed the process when they went back on duty.

'My brothers and sister used to bring back lovely presents. That wasn't allowed! The customs station was at Omeath. The train slowed down as it approached and we opened the carriage window furthest away from the platform, reached out and secreted goods on the roof. There was a little ridge running alongside of the roof to prevent water falling on passengers. It was very useful in keeping stuff from falling off! We retrieved our parcels once the train had been searched, the customs had got off, the train began to gather speed for its onward journey and we all breathed a sigh of relief!'

Jim Taylor was born in Belfast in May 1945, two days after VE Day (Victory in Europe) so he just missed the war. His father worked for Harland and Wolff as a boilermaker and his mum was a housewife. Like most working-class families, money was scarce and food, clothing, tobacco and so on, were in short supply or rationed.

At that time the border was controlled by customs, who could fine you or confiscate your purchases. Jim remembers, 'going shopping when I was a 6-year-old with my mum and Aunt Betty. We got the train to Dundalk and spent the day browsing in the shops. Mum had an old shopping bag with old gabardine overcoat in it and a pair of bloomers, which seemed strange because she wanted to buy new things. The design of women's underwear has changed radically since I was young. Women wore huge knickers with elasticated legs that stretched down to their knees!

'She bought a lot of small items and yards of curtain material. On the return journey, about ten minutes from the customs checkpoint, she took her extra pair of bloomers out of her bag, stepped into them, filled them up with small goods and pulled them up under her skirt. She hid the curtain material by winding it around my waist and chest, securing it with string and dressing me in the overcoat, which was about four sizes too big. I must have looked like Billy Bunter! The carriage had bench seats and I was squeezed into a corner to hide me from the customs men looking for illegal merchandise. I often wonder what they thought of the little fat boy sweating in the corner seat!

'One Sunday, Mum, **Aunt Betty Kerr** (née Lyttle) and I went on a bus run to Drogheda, with my young twin sisters, May and Alberta.

'Drogheda had a market every Sunday. We went on a trip organised by Albert Street Presbyterian Church.

'We took a UTA (Ulster Transport Authority) bus to the border, where we had to change buses. On the way home we changed buses again at the

border. My twin sisters, May and Alberta, were sitting 6in higher in their pushchairs because they had Hafner's sausages, cigarettes and material piled under them, neatly covered by their blankets. I had material wrapped round me under my oversized coat, while Mum and Aunt Betty were wearing several jumpers with nylons hidden in their bloomers under their skirts! Thankfully we arrived home with our goods intact and we really enjoyed our Hafner's sausages!'

Jim Taylor's mother, May. (Printed with kind permission of Jim Taylor)

George Wilson, who lives between Gilford and Portadown, describes how Sunday School trips were used as a cover for smuggling. He says, 'I used to love going on Sunday school trips organised by the local churches once a year on a Saturday afternoon. I went with my mother. All the women on the bus wore two pairs of gigantic, knee-hugging knickers. They'd no intention of staying in Warrenpoint. They caught the ferry across the border to Omeath, went shopping and filled their knickers full of cigarettes, tobacco, small items of clothing and anything else they could fit in! The boys were left behind in Warrenpoint because their mothers didn't want the extra expense of taking them across on the ferry, so we enjoyed an afternoon's freedom. Cars were few and far between, so a church outing was the only time we got to the seaside. We used to go and sit on top of a high wall near the harbour and watch the ferry going back and forward.

'When the women arrived back in Warrenpoint they waddled along the harbour in a peculiar fashion and kept looking behind to see if they were being followed by the revenue men. They weren't in the least bit worried by us boys sitting on top of the wall. We loved to watch the women hitch up their skirts, pull the elastic of their knickers out and put what they'd bought into shopping baskets for the bus journey home. As for the older boys and girls, on the journey home they hoped to pair up and snog in the back seat of the bus!'

George Wilson. (Printed with kind permission of George Wilson)

George adds, 'Smuggling was done in many ways. I know a man who lives in Warrenpoint. He told me his mother had a pram with a false bottom that was very useful for smuggling. He doesn't know how his family could have survived the war without his mother's shopping trips in Omeath.

'Lorries were loaded with bales of hay. They looked innocent but had loads of butter and/or meal hidden in the middle. During and after the war we wouldn't have had enough meal to feed pigs and hens if it hadn't been for smuggling.

'Sometimes when I was lying in bed at night, I heard a smuggler's lorry being chased by the revenue men. There's a small road that goes past my house. The customs men didn't know about it and it allowed lorries that were being chased to "disappear". I smiled when I heard them passing my house!

'The smugglers often used unapproved roads across the border the revenue men didn't know existed because they weren't local. Smugglers who were caught had their vans impounded. A friend whose van was impounded at Newry hired my father's for several months and continued smuggling.

'My cousin, at the age of 10 years, used the Sunday School trip to make money. He spent the day travelling back and forwards on the ferry, buying cigarettes and selling them to men in Warrenpoint. He grew up to be a businessman, so his early smuggling experience helped equip him for a successful, honest career. Another friend had a promising smuggling career cut short when the revenue men raided his house and discovered tins of corn beef stacked under his bed.'

Perhaps the most ingenious way of smuggling has been described by **Bobby Evans**. He has a 91-year-old friend, who lives in Newry and wants his name kept secret because he doesn't want his family to know what he got up to! During the war he cycled from Newry across the border to Dundalk, where he let the air out of his tyres and filled them up with whiskey. Then he cycled home and sold the whiskey to American troops. When asked if the whiskey tasted of rubber he replied, 'I don't know. It didn't matter if it did. The Americans didn't know what whiskey tasted like. All they wanted was a good strong alcoholic drink!'

Military personnel were not allowed to cross the border into the neutral South, so they dressed in civilian clothes and ignored their orders. B.R. Christie, an English officer, described Bundoran as a place of escape with well-stocked shops, cigarettes and chocolates, and he watched, with amusement, the half-hearted way the customs searched for smuggled goods. The war appeared a long way away.

Jane Elliott (née Burns) was born in Enniskillen in 1921. She writes, 'There was a black market for sugar, tea, coffee alcohol, dried fruit and butter from the Republic as there are many islands on the lough between Enniskillen and the border and the train service ran from Enniskillen to Bundoran. Train passengers and any boats were searched regularly by the customs. There were naval boats on the lough to prevent smuggling and terrorism. My uncle was asked to assist with directions to ensure they did not cross the border as the River Erne rose in the republic; he had good local knowledge. He had an open rowing boat and a larger boat with an engine and was out frequently at night checking water bailiffs were doing patrols before the war. Few people fished in the areas the Army or Navy patrolled during the war. The unlicensed anglers tried the local rivers.'

Garnet Chambers recounts another type of smuggling. 'Fuel for fires was in short supply. Coal was rationed to a hundred-weight a week, as far as I can recall, and, if you were lucky, you might get one bag of slack. Cutting down trees was not permitted, though they could be lightly branched. There was an old plantation with the remains of six houses across the fields from our house. (The place has been wiped out by the development of the Boulevard Shopping Centre.) I remember my father, his brother and a friend going over to this spot after dark. He and I had a walk in the fields on Sunday afternoons. I thought we were just having a pleasant outing. He was reconnoitring the ground for later in the week, looking for suitable branches and "transport routes" to the back of our garden so nothing had to be carried on the road and they wouldn't be spotted.

'The operation was carried out in late autumn, or winter, when it was dark shortly after six. As soon as the conditions were right the three men went off to what was in effect a small wood. Branches were interpreted to be anything up to 6 or 7in thick.

'There were no chainsaws in those days, only crosscut and bow saws. Work started and all the outside work had to be carried out in complete darkness because you were not allowed to show any light outside because it would have betrayed the presence of houses to the enemy if there was an air raid. Then there was the job of keeping it hidden and getting it back. Over the fields they came. One went in front with the end of a log on each shoulder, the other end carried by one of his two companions, who carried more wood in his free hand. This loading had to be changed round every hundred yards or so. They had to negotiate ditches and hedges over a distance of about half a mile to bring the "booty" into our garden without going on the road. They carefully put it into our hen house in complete darkness. Then they went back for the remainder. My father said his friend swore there had been more than what was left. The only conclusion they could come to was that somebody had seen them in "action", waited until they were away with the first load and gathered as much as they could carry away in the opposite direction.

'I wanted to go with them but my mother vetoed this, saying I might fall into a ditch. My father told my mother it was a good job I hadn't gone as when his friend, Billy, discovered that some of their hard work had been stolen his language had been very picturesque! He said, "It was a good thing Garnet didn't hear it." I had been sent to bed about nine o'clock. I only became aware of what was going on over the next few days when I couldn't collect eggs as I usually did because the hen house was locked.

'Over the next week or so our house was like a timber store. After dark logs were brought into the kitchen and the three men sawed and split blocks. The other two bagged them and carried them home over the bar of their bicycles.

'My mother had to put up with all this, though she got all the sawdust and chippings for the fire. She had to provide tea, but said it was in a good cause.'

Margaret Graham and her family never smuggled across the border but she got a forbidden pound of butter each week by carrying an empty buttermilk jug out of Banbridge and along the road to friends, who lived on a nearby farm. They placed the butter in the jug, then covered it with buttermilk that was allowed.

Rosie Hickey writes, 'My mother **Elizabeth Hickey** told me my granny, **Mary-Anne McCrum** and my **Auntie Gertie** went to Dublin for the day and smuggled butter back home. In those days women always wore hats and when the customs boarded the train at the border granny hid the butter under her hat. But the train got terribly hot and the customs men spent a long time searching the train. Granny was old and forgetful at that stage, and kept saying to my aunt, "Gertie I'm awfully hot here, do you think anyone would mind if I took my hat off?" So my Aunt Gertie had to spend the trip trying to persuade her to keep her hat on without saying, "You can't take your hat off! You've got a pound of butter under it!" When they eventually did get home they found the butter had melted and they had a terrible time getting it out of Granny's hair.'

Smuggling

Florence Chambers recounts, 'Fuel was very scarce. Agricultural petrol came from Russia and was dyed red so it could be identified if used in cars. My uncle, **Billy Carlisle**, and a relative, who wishes to be nameless, used the know-how of a nephew (who learned it in his science lessons) to take the dye out of fuel, using a condenser to leave a clear petrol. To avoid any suspicion of laundered fuel it was mixed with some of the authentic allowances at his brother-in-law's home in the country. The smell of this might have raised the authorities' suspicion, so neighbours were on sentry duty to watch out for the police patrolling on their bicycles. The farm was perched on top of a hill, so it was easy to spot anyone on the road.

'Smuggling was rife from Southern Ireland as they were neutral during the war. Stories abound of folks travelling by bus or train and transporting food items which were unavailable over the border, but scarce in the North. Uncle Billy was a bit of a spiv and so had stashed Waterford crystal dessert dishes in the front of his horsebox near the horses' heads. Once he was challenged and a search was to follow, but he said that the horses were vicious and would kick all around. He got away with that excuse and the customs officers retreated. I grew up looking at those wonderful dishes in our china cupboard.

'Sometimes my Aunt Lily Carlisle drove the lorry. Once she broke down about 5 miles from home. She was quite close to her eldest brother's home and, although they were in bed, she opened their garage and drove their car to her home. She knew what was wrong with the engine, got her tools and fixed the problem. She had a few hours' sleep in the middle of this escapade, returned the car to its rightful place, and called into her brother's home to tell them what she had done during the night.'

JR, who lived in Sion Mills during the war, writes, 'There was a shop beside our local church and I'm sure 80 per cent of their goods were smuggled over the border from Donegal

'A man from Newtownstewart used to store the smuggled goods in the outhouse at the farm and would have taken then in smaller quantities up to Newtownstewart to sell to houses. He took the saddle off the bicycle and hid tobacco in the frame.

'Goods were smuggled in both directions depending on their prices. Money was scarce so it was worth smuggling even if there wasn't much difference in the price.'

9

Military Camps

There was no conscription in Ireland, North or South. The South was determined not to become involved in the war and to maintain neutrality. The North is an integral part of the United Kingdom, so one would expect conscription to apply, however the government decided not to do so because that could cause difficulties with those members of the community who did not feel any affiliation with Britain. Nevertheless, people from both the South and the North joined up, Protestants, Catholics, Southerners and Northerners, in their thousands. They could see the evil Hitler represented and the harm he was doing to democracy, so they signed up to fight him regardless of local politics and affiliations.

George Beattie was born and lived in Greenore, County Louth, during the war. He was the youngest of five children. He was born in 1932, so was too young to join up when war was declared on 1 September 1939. Brother Ferris was born in 1929, so he was also too young to go to war, but three of their older siblings joined the British forces and fought.

'The fact that Greenore is in the South caused difficulties for two of my brothers, and my sister, when they joined the British armed forces. If they'd come home on leave wearing their uniforms they'd have been arrested and incarcerated in the prisoner-of-war camp at the Curragh. David and Ruth played safe; they left home in civilian garb and changed into uniform in a friend's house in Newry. Brother **Sammy Beattie** was more daring. He came home wearing his long, camel-coloured overcoat that hid his uniform. He usually went back to his regiment by a different route than the others. Instead of returning to Newry on the train and crossing the Irish Sea via a ferry from the North he used the Greenore–Holyhead route. Strictly speaking it had ceased to be a passenger ferry and just carried livestock and cargo, but it could, by special arrangement, carry ten passengers. As we lived in Greenore we knew all the sailors and it was very easy for Sammy to book a passage across to Holyhead.

'My elder brother **David Beattie** went to England and joined the Royal Navy in 1937. Years earlier a lovely couple from Birkenhead had decided they wanted to go to Greenore, so they caught the ferry across. There was only one hotel, The Railway Hotel. It was full and somebody suggested my mother's sons had left home and she might put them up. She did, and the two families became friends. David stayed with them while he signed up and it was there that he met Charlie. I don't know Charlie's surname. He was always simply called Charlie. He was a wee man and David was very tall and they signed up on the same day and became the best of friends. They trained as gunners, served on HMS *Warspite*, survived several battles and manned the same gun, but at different times. If Charlie was on the gun, David was sleeping and vice versa. During the Battle of Crete, David was manning the gun and Charlie was sleeping. *Warspite* was bombed by Italian aircraft and badly damaged, so it was out of action for six months. It was David's turn to man the gun during the battle and he was unscathed but unfortunately Charlie was killed as he lay in his bunk. David, who was demobbed in 1945, was devastated at the loss of his best friend. Earlier during the war they made an arrangement and gave each other letters to be delivered to their next of kin should one of them be killed and the other survive. I remember David coming home on leave, then returning to England for a few days to deliver Charlie's letter to his parents.

'My sister, **Ruth Beattie**, joined the Women's Auxiliary Air Force (WAAF). and fell in love with **Tommy Easton**, an Australian rear-gunner on a Lancaster bomber. Tommy was shot down over Germany in 1943. To Ruth's great relief, he managed to eject from his plane, landed safely and was taken as a prisoner of war to Stalag Luft 3.

'**Samuel** was too young to sign up at the beginning of the war, so he joined the Airforce Training Corps in Newry and wore a white flash in his hat denoting he was waiting to be called up. He was delighted when he was able to go to war in 1944 and he was demobbed in 1945.

'**Ferris**, like me, was too young to go to war. He trained as an electrician and still lives in the South.

'Greenore was built as a port to service the business traffic between Belfast and London. It was a small village with only thirty houses. Twenty-eight of the families, like me, weren't interested in politics. Two families were Nationalists and flew the tricolour on holidays and anniversaries, but I'd like to stress it was a happy place and we all got on extremely well.

'I remember going down to the ferry terminal and waving goodbye to Sammy as he stood on the deck. Shortly after that the garda raided our house because somebody told them it contained a British forces uniform. They gave the place a right going over but thankfully didn't find a single thing apart from a stack of brown paper. People always saved paper and recycled it. We used it to send food parcels to England. The garda asked my mother why she had all that paper and she said, "That's for the children to back their school books!" We were very hurt to think that one of our neighbours must have betrayed us. We never knew who it was but strongly suspected it was one of the Nationalist families.

'I travelled by train each day to school in Newry. I didn't think anything of it at the time but I often saw what appeared to me to be very tall men wearing long overcoats coming off my train and going to an office in Newry Railway Station. In retrospect I believe they were British forces who lived in the South and were claiming their free travel passes back to their regiments.'

During the Second World War there were more military personnel living in Northern Ireland than the native population. The roads were narrow and

Road in County Fermanagh in 1941. (Photograph by Bill Henry)

winding and the actions of Army trucks and tanks proved very dangerous. There were many accidents, including the one described by **Jane Elliott** (née Burns), who lived in Enniskillen. She was born in 1921 and has vivid memories of the war. 'In 1942 my aunt, who was walking to catch a bus home to Irvinestown, was pinned against the bank near Kilgortnaleague Bridge by a large American Army lorry. It drove on but the second lorry in the convoy stopped and had her taken to hospital in Enniskillen. The police informed me at the hotel, and I went to see her, and she was fully alert and worried about a hen due to hatch eggs. She died from internal injuries that evening. The roads were narrow, and the drivers had little regard for other road users.'

Jimmy (Jimbo Conway) lives in Lurgan and records, 'Before the present troubles Lurgan was a close, tight-knit community that was very upset by the death of **Joseph Curran**, the son of **John and Mary Curran**, of Ballynamoney, Lurgan. He was a childhood pal and close friend of my mother. They both came from the rural townland of Ballynamoney near Lurgan. He was killed in action over Germany. His name has been recently added to Lurgan War Memorial. Sergeant (Flight Engineer) Joseph Curran, Service Number 1045746, was 20 years old and serving with 428 Squadron, Royal Canadian Air Force. He was killed in action on 23 September 1943 on board a Handley Page Halifax flying from RAF Middleton St George near Durham that was shot down 10km south-west of Mayen at 5,400m. The aircraft crashed into woodland at Hahnenberg near Kötterichen, Germany, with the loss of all on board.

'A few Lurgan people ended up in surprising places. **Father McMullan** was appointed assistant pastor at the Cathedral in Reno, Nevada, on 28 February 1943, with the permission of the most Rev. Ordinary. During the build up to D-Day, Father Alf, as he was known locally, was appointed by the War Department as a full-time chaplain at Reno Army Air Base with the rank of captain in the United States Army Air Force, and he was granted American citizenship on 4 June 1943. He administered and prepared American youth for the Air Force contribution to the war over Europe. As for my parents and grandmother, the American and Belgian soldiers brought the wider world into their little rural corner of Silverwood. They enjoyed feeding the Belgians and teaching them English.'

Jane Elliott (née Burns) (see above) records, 'In the 1930s and early 1940s I lived in Enniskillen near the Diamond with my great-aunt, my uncle and youngest sister in the Lough Erne Hotel and café. My parents and other siblings lived on a farm near Trory, beside the future St Angelo airport. My great aunt ran the hotel, my uncle worked for the fisheries protection on the lough and my sister was at school until 1949. Staff came in daily except Sunday to do various tasks.

'I left school in 1937 and worked in the hotel learning all the duties involved. Most of the residents worked in Enniskillen and came in Monday evening and returned home on Friday evening to areas around the county with limited public transport. Other residents came for a few days on business trips such as cloth salesmen and the judge's crier. No alcohol was served on the premises. Breakfast was at 8 to 9 for the residents. The door was open at 9 a.m. for local trade, dinner at 1 p.m., the evening meal at 6 p.m. and we closed at 7 p.m. There was a steady stream of people in because they were at the pig market nearby or waiting to go home on buses from the Diamond.

'In 1939 the war was declared on a Sunday morning and was no surprise. The neighbours told us it was declared as they had electricity in their premises. The hotel was all town gas (one of the residents worked for the gas company and stayed regularly to check on the gas works in Enniskillen) and they had no radio. The *Belfast Telegraph* was bought every evening. My great-aunt was a deeply religious Methodist and we attended the church regularly, as we did that morning at 11.30 a.m. It was announced in church at the service.

'The local halls were requisitioned, including the Methodist hall, and soldiers were billeted in them. The regiments were from England and the Army personnel never said where they were stationed, their duties or where they were being sent and nobody asked. Fermanagh is a border county and many families had moved from the republic in the 1920s to settle.

'Rationing was introduced quite quickly. Our neighbour was the butcher who supplied the meat, and he owned a farm outside the town where he reared beef animals for the shop. We had a steady supply of beef during the war. The hotel had to know in advance the number of regulars for dinner each day. A local farmer churned butter and we bought buttermilk and the odd pound from him as we were restricted to 4oz of butter each per week. Certain groups in the town decided to provide tea, coffee and sandwiches for the Army when they were off duty. The YMCA hall in Regal Pass was used to serve the food. The hotel was asked to cater for it after some time of opening. I prepared the various sandwich contents (ham, egg and onion and lettuce) and left it down for local groups to make them up as the bread and dry goods were delivered directly to the hall by a local shop. This was at 3.30 p.m. each day for 4 p.m. opening until 10.30. This lasted for about a year, during which several regiments came to the town and left. A major of one regiment came and stayed in the hotel with his wife. He and she were middle aged and had no family. She had worked in a chemist and had a good knowledge of drugs. He ate in the officers' mess in the White Hart of Town-hall Street and came to stay with her when off duty. They had a bedroom and sitting room. The major went shooting and provided pheasants for the hotel to prepare.

'They led quite a social life and invited local dignitaries in for drinks or food. The hotel provided the dinner for the guests. They respected the owner's views on alcohol. The guests tended to be church ministers, local doctors and landowners, so nothing rowdy. There was a bomb left three doors down from the hotel at a newsagent and sweet shop. It exploded and damaged several windows opposite and the shop front. The siren went off and the locals came out into the street. There were no street lights and the blackout rules were in force at the time. It was revealed later the shop had received a warning from Republican sources about selling a certain newspaper, I cannot recall the name of the paper.

'American soldiers and airmen came into town regularly for steaks and coffee. Few wanted to eat potatoes with it and they often made a steak sandwich. Money was made during the war serving meals, despite the rationing.'

British Soldiers

British soldiers were stationed in Northern Ireland from the beginning of the war. Irish people are normally generous and friendly, so they made the military welcome. What happened in Banbridge is typical of what happened throughout the North of Ireland when efforts were made to entertain the troops.

In Banbridge there was a building housing the YMCA at the bottom of Bridge Street. It was manned by local ladies, who dished out tea, coffee, sandwiches and cakes to everyone present. **Ella Brown** remembers her aunt, **Mary Dixon**, helping with the work involved.

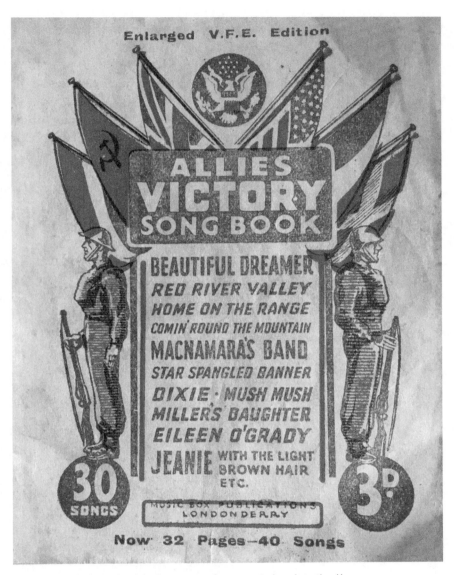

Forces song book. (Printed with kind permission of Margaret Graham (née Shaw))

The troops were invited to Saturday night dances, where **Lily Willie** played the piano and they had sing-songs. Everyone was supplied with a song book and the late **Francie Shaw** gave her copy to her daughter **Margaret Graham (née Shaw)**, who treasures it.

Social functions provided the opportunity for the troops to meet local girls. Many fell in love and married, and some long-lasting friendships began during that time.

Margaret Shaw was an only child. She lived with her parents, **Douglas** and **Frances Shaw**, in Dromore Street, Banbridge. She remembers a prisoner-of-war camp that stretched from the bottom of Ballymoney Hill through to the Lurgan Road, including the campus that now contains Banbridge Nursery, Edenderry Primary School, and Banbridge Academy. Margaret used to talk through the barbed wire on Ballymoney Hill to a soldier, **John Abernethy**, who she described as 'being in clink'. She told him it was going to be her birthday in a few days' time.

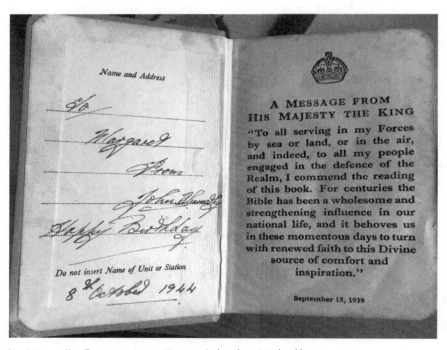

Inscription on New Testament given to Margaret Graham by a British soldier.
(Margaret Graham, née Shaw)

Jimmy Feeney, a British soldier.
(Margaret Graham, née Shaw)

Postcard sent to Shaw family by Jimmy
Feeney. (Margaret Graham, née Shaw)

John must have grown fond of her because he wanted to give her a birthday present. He couldn't do that because he was incarcerated and he told an army chaplain. The chaplain gave John a copy of the New Testament that was issued to the troops. John signed it, wishing Margaret a happy birthday. The chaplain visited Margaret's home and delivered it, where it is still a much-loved possession.

The Shaw family also made friends with **Jimmy Feeney** and Margaret still has the photograph he gave them. When he was posted abroad he sent the family postcards of the places he had been and Margaret still has them.

Margaret recounts, 'One day American soldiers visited the school and the curtains separating the classes (See Chapter 1 Education) were pushed back so all the children could both see and hear the visitors. I don't know what they said but I do remember they gave us all sweets and we sang for them.'

In 1940 children were asked to bring a small amount of money into school. Margaret thinks it was 'something like a penny', so they could send money to help people living in China. The children were given a stamp to show they had contributed and Margaret still has hers.

The late **Airey Neave** MP was stationed in Banbridge during the war. He left the town in December 1939 with the 1st Battalion of the Rifle Brigade. He survived the war but was killed by an IRA bomb fitted under his Vauxhall Cavalier car at 2.58 p.m. on 30 March 1979 as he drove out of the Palace of Westminster. Many of Banbridge's older residents were terribly upset because he was regarded as 'one of ours'.

A stamp sold to help Chinese children.
(Margaret Graham, née Shaw)

Lisa Rawlins says, 'My grandfather, **Sergeant Jack Lacey**, was born in the Elephant and Castle area of London. He arrived in Banbridge, along with the Royal Green Jackets, at the beginning of the war and was based in an Army camp along Castlewellan Road. Their target practice was the stone wall along the Rathfriland Road and the marks can still be seen there today.

'Granda was what could be described as tall, dark and handsome. He was tall at 6ft 2in and a devout Catholic, who regularly attended Mass in St Patrick's Church on the Dromore Road, Banbridge. That was where he first met my granny, **Elizabeth Porter**, known as **Lily**. They must have fancied each other because granny told me they kept looking at each other! One thing led to another, they started going out together, he proposed and they got married on 3 April 1940 in the church where they had first met. They were heartbroken to be separated after three happy days together as he was posted to France. Poor Granny didn't know if she'd ever see her husband again. Luckily she had a large supportive family, but she must have been out of her mind with worry when she heard Grandpa was in the middle of the horror that was Dunkirk.

'Granny was very relieved, but upset at the same time, when she was told Granda'd been captured outside Calais, where he'd been working on the supply line bringing necessities to the front line. She realised that being a prisoner of war was no joke but at least hadn't been killed or wounded, and thought, "He's still alive, and that's the main thing!"

'My granny had very good reasons to be worried as 68,000 British soldiers were either killed, wounded or captured – when they didn't go missing – between 10 May and 22 June 1940. For every seven soldiers who escaped through Dunkirk, one man was left behind as a prisoner of war – Jack was one of them. Many prisoners of war were murdered, in cold blood, by the Germans, so my grandad was lucky to have been captured by honourable soldiers. He was forced to march, along with hundreds of other prisoners, the long distance to Stalag X-B, a German prisoner-of-war camp near Sandbostel, Lower Saxony in north-western Germany. He was held there for five years, although he was so keen to get back to his new bride he managed to escape three times. His first two attempts ended in failure. He was recaptured and shot in both legs as a deterrent to making a third attempt. He received Red Cross parcels and good medical treatment. His legs healed and then he made his third attempt at escaping. This time he was successful.' (See Chapter 10.)

Jason Diamond (see Chapter 3) recounts, 'Arthur Sinton was the second son of **Frederick Buckby Sinton**, a member of the Sinton linen family of Banford Bleachworks, now the Potbelly Restaurant, Tullylish. Arthur was best friends with **Ted Lamont** whose family owned the well-known Ballymena linen firm Samuel Lamont & Sons. [Founded in 1835, by the man whose name it bears, Samuel Lamont & Sons Ltd became one of Northern Ireland's foremost linen weavers.]

'When war broke out Arthur joined a searchlight unit stationed in Belfast and on 2 May 1940, Second Lieutenant Arthur Buckby Sinton of the Royal Artillery married **Vera Wilson Smyth** of the Brookfield linen dynasty. Arthur was involved with the evacuation of the British Expeditionary Force from Dunkirk. However, as Arthur's widow (by the time I got to know her she had remarried and was **Mrs Vera Stephenson**) related to me, there wasn't enough happening for Arthur in the Army and he transferred to the RAF. Sadly in 1943 Flying Officer Arthur Sinton's plane was reported missing. The body of his gunner was washed ashore and buried in Amsterdam, but Arthur's body was never found.

'The day before Arthur was reported as missing his father, Fred, had a massive heart attack and died, the family having to pay double death duties. Vera recalled that she and the family had returned from a holiday in Portrush or Portstewart. They were met at Portadown station by their chauffeur, **Mayes**, who broke the news to them that "Master Arthur" had been reported missing. Vera said that she knew straight away that he was dead, but that his mother never accepted it, living in the hope that he had survived and been taken prisoner. Vera said it was very difficult to get closure as they never had a body to grieve over. Arthur is commemorated on the Gilford War Memorial.

'Meanwhile, a cousin of Arthur's, **Henry Albert Uprichard** of the Uprichards of the Springvale Bleachworks at Halls Mill (a family that had come over to the Lurgan area from Wales in the eighteenth century), had joined the Northern Irish Horse. The Uprichard family were well known for their expertise with horses, especially in the hunting field, so it was no surprise that Albert joined this unit. However, by this stage the horses had been replaced with tanks and armoured cars! From there Albert volunteered for airborne forces and enlisted in No. 2 (Parachute) Commando in August 1940, which was redesignated as 11 SAS Battalion later that year.

'Albert told me that part of their training consisted of going up in a balloon in the dark, with a hole in the centre of the basket. Once the balloon had reached the desired height he and his fellow paratroopers had to jump through the hole. He said it was a bit frightening as you were jumping into complete darkness.'

Garnet Chambers, who lives in Banbridge, records, 'At the end of the Bannview Road, Banbridge, where Beechlands is now situated, was then two fields. These had been taken over by the Army for training purposes. There was a shooting range and we could hear a lot of noise at times. There was also a deep pit and I was told later that this was used for hand grenade practice. Trenches were dug and small tanks were driven over these when soldiers were in them. My father told me that it was to get the soldiers used to this when they were fighting. The soldiers did route marches all over the country in all kinds of weather.

'Sometimes there were mock battles or at least raids. One night in winter my father was going to Russell's farm, which was about three fields behind our house, to get buttermilk for my mother to bake. She, with me in tow, would usually have gone over the fields during the day but there had been a lot of rain and the ground was soaking wet. This is where the Outlet or Boulevard shopping malls are now built. My father went on the bicycle up the main Newry Road and then along what is now Cascum Road.

US soldiers march to billet having arrived in Northern Ireland in 1941. (Printed with kind permission of Brownlow House Museum)

There was total blackout then, of course, and a lamp on the bicycle gave no light other than to let it be seen that someone was coming. There was a hill, now wiped away by new roads, and he was walking up it in the darkness. The only noise was the rattle of his empty cans on the handlebars. He said later that he had a sort of a feeling that he was not alone but when a firm hand gripped his shoulder he nearly fainted. Was it a ghost? An English voice at his ear said in a loud whisper, "Sorry, just carry on and quietly." Just then a gap appeared in the clouds and vaguely in the moonlight he could see lines of figures going silently along each side of the road. He did carry on and though he was on a hill he said that he jumped on the bicycle and went over the hill like the proverbial bullet. He learned a few days later that it had been an Army exercise. One group of soldiers were "attacking" an old rath known locally as Roger's Fort. They must have been wearing rubber-soled boots as they were not making a sound. He said that made it all the more eerie. They may even have been Commandos but anyhow they were successful in capturing the fort, as locals were able to report. People living near did hear a lot of shooting, which likely was blanks.'

American Soldiers

At the end of 1941 the USA came into the war and early in 1942 American troops began to arrive. Northern Ireland was the first place they arrived in Europe. **Garnet Chambers** says, 'I think some were billeted at Scarva Demesne and some at White's in Loughbrickland. They visited the Abercorn School and probably other local schools. I suppose it was to lift morale and let locals become better acquainted with them. Anyhow, they gave out sweets and chewing gum. I had not started school but one of our neighbours brought me some. Sweets were rationed, of course. I seem to recall that the ration was 2oz a week if you were lucky but the way the "Yanks" handed them out there seemed to be an inexhaustible supply available. Chewing gum was something that had only been heard of.

'I can remember being at Dunbar's Bridge and watching tanks being driven back and forth in a shallow part of the river at the ford. I am not sure whether they were British or American tanks but somebody said that they were being washed. Quite a crowd of people were gathering to see and they certainly put on a good show.

'A school friend of my father was in the Royal Navy and I remember him visiting us when he was on leave. He had been in the Far East before the war and could tell of seeing children's bodies floating down one of the big Chinese rivers. During the war one of his ships was the battleship HMS *Duke of York*, which sank the German battlecruiser *Scharnhorst* off the coast of Norway just after Christmas 1943. He was telling my father about service on as he called it "the York". He had been a crewman on it for a couple of years and he said his big regret was that he was in hospital on shore when the action with the *Scharnhorst* took place. He had missed one of the last big ship battles of the war, which had also included HMS *Belfast*.'

Jay recounts, 'When American soldiers began to arrive, some were billeted in our house. They decided to fling open the venerable sash windows, not realising the invisible cords were very frail, and the windows immediately crashed down, shedding their glass panes as they fell. This being wartime, glass was unobtainable and so the windows in the two bedrooms sported wooden panes for years. Apart from that, our Americans coped very well.

'As we lived near the main road to Crumlin, we sometimes saw convoys of Army lorries passing their way to Langford Lodge, and at night I lay in bed and listened to the drone of American bombers coming in to land at Langford Lodge. They made a lonely sound, like that of the wood pigeons in the nearby trees, but more mournful.'

Margaret and William Hillis live near Katesbridge, in Elmdale on the family farm William inherited from his parents. William Hillis recounts, 'I was between 4 and 5 years of age when American soldiers arrived and were billeted in an empty house on my family farm.

'The house had very spacious rooms and soldiers slept in it and in the outhouses connected with the old property and they cooked in the kitchen.

'I don't know how many soldiers lived on the farm. There were a lot and I remember them eating and having a bit of craic at a long table outside.

'We'd a very good rapport with the Americans. They were very friendly and very generous. I loved their chewing gum and sweets and found their tanks fascinating. They were huge, much bigger than the British ones. I'll never forget how kind the Americans were to me and I treasure a helmet they left behind.

'One day one of the Americans asked me if I'd like a ride in a tank? I'm telling you he didn't have to ask me twice! He took me right to the end of our driveway, away along the road and back home again. It was a thrill

American helmet and comb. (Printed with kind permission of William Hills)

of a lifetime for a wee boy. They were packing up to go to war at the time (I presume they took part in the D–Day landings) and we never saw them again. I've often wondered what happened to them? Were they wounded, or killed, or did they manage to get home safely?

'Our Americans wrote their names on the walls. We redecorated their rooms and I'm sorry nobody thought of taking a note of the names. I remember one of them came from Chicago and one left his comb behind. He must have dropped it and we found it under the floorboards. We still have it and there's a number printed on it – Reserve 18004311234POL3 and on the back it says, "American Army: Part of what you earn is pride." I wonder who owned that?

'I know American roads are long, wide and straight, so our narrow, bendy roads were an ideal training ground for going into battle in Europe. In those days you might come round a corner and meet a cow, or a horse, or a few sheep, or a flock of hens or ducks wandering about. Army manoeuvres were a nuisance as far as civilians were concerned. They caused many accidents and traffic jams caused by soldiers returning to camp after Army exercises and so on. Of course, our American soldiers weren't the only ones because we had British, Polish, and Belgium soldiers here by the end of the war.

American soldiers and a local family. (Printed with kind permission of Brownlow House Museum)

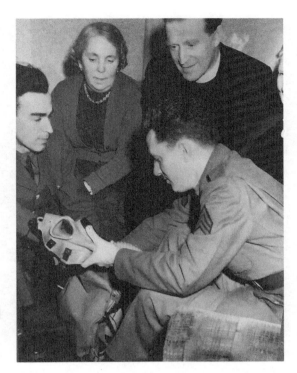

Below: photograph printed with kind permission of Adrian Hack, who restored this Jeep

A typical country cottage. (Photograph by Bill Henry)

'I read that approximately 300,000 American military personnel were based in or passed through Northern Ireland between January 1942 and the end of the war. At one point United States military personnel made up one-tenth of Northern Ireland's population! They were welcome, in spite of the inconvenience, because we thought they'd help bring the war to an end. About 2,000 women became GI brides and began a new life in America after the war, and I'll never forget "our" special Americans and after all these years I still wonder what happened to them.'

Jane Elliott (née Burns) records, 'An aerodrome, St Angelo Airport, was built during the war near Trory as the land is flat and close to Lough Erne. My family lived nearby and drew stones by horse and cart for men to lay the runway. Part of the runway crossed the main road at Trory and when planes were due to land the road was closed in both directions. When planes flew in, the aircrew waved to my family as they passed close to the front of the farmhouse. In the summer of 1943, I was staying for the weekend at the farmhouse at Tullyavey beside the aerodrome. On a Sunday evening seven planes arrived safely from America and the eighth was circling and could not see where to land. Flares and a small plane went up to guide him, but he was unable to follow and crossed the runway and crashed into the river. I and the whole family were out of the house and up a hill as we could see and hear the racket. It was not dark or foggy. An inquiry was held as the plane was wrecked. The pilot blamed the position of the farmhouse blocking his view and it was ordered to be demolished. The family had to move out in August 1944 and the house and farm sheds were tossed. The authorities gave them a choice of houses, which were either too far from the farmland or had no byres for cattle. They moved to the house and small farm near Irvinestown as it had a byre for milk cows. The residence had belonged to the aunt who was killed in 1942 in an accident involving an American truck (see above). An English Air Force man and his wife and baby stayed with them for a short time until he was posted. His wife worked in the family bakery and shared lots of recipes with the family. When the compensation came through for the house and farm buildings, they bought another farm near the land they owned beside the aerodrome and moved to it in 1945.'

Bridgeen Rutherford recounts the love affair between her **Aunt Maureen** (**Maureen Wood**, née McHugh, 1923–2001) and **Mel Wood**. She writes, 'My aunt Maureen was one of eleven children. She received her formative education at age 3 at Waterside Girls School and Buncrana Convent School. Her education was cut short as she was needed back home to help her mother while my granny tended the bar. She owned the Clooney Bar in the Waterside area of Derry. It was a public bar.

'Mel Wood was in the US Army Reserves from June 1941 to 10 August 1942. He was involved in field and office work on the layout and construction of the US Navy bases in Northern Ireland and was in direct charge of the drafting room and survey parties. Mel was ordered to active duty on 10 August 1942. While working in Derry he was a second lieutenant but was promoted to first lieutenant during the period of active duty in the Army Corps of Engineers. He was one of 362 "civilian technicians" who arrived in Derry on 30 June 1941. This number had doubled by Christmas of that year.

'The engineers came to Derry to hire locals and one of the locals was my uncle **Aidan MacHugh**. This was the only time allegedly in modern history that there was full employment in Derry. Uncle Aidan worked in the family bar as well as having a job with the "Yanks". Mel Wood and a friend happened upon the bar one night, Aidan was behind the bar and they knew him from the camp. Some of the clientele were allowed to have a drink in the bar kitchen, which was also Granny's home kitchen. Mel and his friend were and that is where he met Aidan's sister, Maureen.

'The "civilian technicians" were not in uniform on arrival but on the day after the Pearl Harbor attack on 7 December 1941 they started wearing their US uniforms. Numerous US facilities were situated in Derry, along with soldiers of all nationalities.'

John Kelley writes, 'To the North of Strabane there is a mountain called Knockavoe. This mountain is on the flight path between the Finn River and Derry/Ballykelly. During the war the military forces built an underground station, which was manned by a service person and had a lamp that could be switched on and off when needed. The purpose of the light was to guide the aeroplanes returning to land at Derry or Ballykelly airports.

'These returning planes were often out guarding the laneways around Ireland, involved in protecting convoys or attacking enemy shipping. The pilots were often tired and wanted assistance to know the route home to the airports.

'As youngsters we used to visit these underground stations and look at the maps and old instruments that were left there. Eventually these were filled in or covered over time.'

Belgian soldiers in Keady Row, Gilford, with the McManus family. (Printed with kind permission of Beryl Higgins)

Belgian Soldiers

Jim (Jimbo) Conway records his mother's memories from Lurgan: 'After the liberation of Belgium in September 1944 the Belgians came to Lurgan. When they first arrived several road signs were erected in French and Flemish to direct the soldiers to their respective camps. These young Belgian men had been resistance or freedom fighters. They were rescued by British troops when they invaded France for the second time. It was to be nearly three weeks before British Army uniforms were given to the Belgians to replace their own clothes.

'Much to our shame, some shopkeepers initially ripped them off after realising they had no concept of the British money, and a poor grasp of English. As time went by locals grew fond of the mild-mannered soldiers. They were soon befriended by many native families and local people still have fond memories of them. Young men from Lurgan may not have been so keen as young local ladies fell for the Belgians. My mother's pal married a Belgian soldier.'

George Nesbitt writes, 'Many Belgian soldiers, who had been deprived of an opportunity to fight the Germans in 1940 – their own army having collapsed within days – were desperate to play their role in liberating Europe.

'Deprived of a national army, they made their way to Britain in their droves following Belgium's liberation in 1944 and Banbridge became home to many of these soldiers. They were part of four brigades of Belgian troops, and had been sent to Northern Ireland for training.

'One of these brigades, the 4th Battalion, was based in fields off the Kilpike Road, in Seapatrick, which now is covered by private housing known as Old Rectory Park. The soldiers' accommodation was in Nissen huts.

'The soldiers only stayed in the area for six to nine months, but very important events unfolded during their stay – victory in Europe, victory in the Pacific, and the soldiers' Independence Day in July.

'Short though their stay was, I was deeply inspired by their enthusiasm. I remember the tanks cavorting about the fields. The soldiers made a great big hole in the ground and practised turning the tanks round and round. I loved watching them marching, lying down and shooting, and getting up again. That was one of the reasons I became a founder member of First Banbridge Boys' Brigade, because I loved marching in the BB, pretending to be a soldier.'

George Nesbitt with plough. (Printed with kind permission of *Banbridge Chronicle*)

George has retained a treasured memento from those wartime days – a trusty plough.

He explained: 'The Belgian soldiers were very industrious and approached my father Robert for his horse and plough, as they wanted to plant potatoes. My father actually ploughed their plot and drilled it ready for the spuds. Our farm was only two fields away from their camp. I was only a schoolboy at the time, but I can remember some sort of party being held there. All the young people of Seapatrick were at their camp – it must have been the first time ever the Belgians had a fish and chips party! They seemed to be a friendly bunch.

'There were a lot of trees about our garden and they had their vehicles hidden there.

'They used to light thunder flashes and many a time they wouldn't go off. One of my schoolmates found a live bullet and took it home. He squeezed it in a vice and the bullet went off – damaging a couple of his fingers!'

Vernon Finlay has recorded his father-in-law's memories: 'The following tragic event happened on the morning of Saturday, 19 July 1941 and is remembered by **Robert Lynn** of Muckamore Antrim, who is in his 98th year at the time of writing. It is recounted here in his own words (Robert was 18 years old at the time):

'A Bristol Blenheim aircraft was coming into land at RAF Aldergrove and collided with something (thought to be a wireless mast). Sadly the three crew members and six female employees at the NAAFI were killed, along with another airman walking nearby. Many others were injured.

'I was working in the quarry beside RAF Aldergrove Airport in July 1941 when I was offered a job as a tractor driver at the York Street Flax Spinning Company at Muckamore. But on a Saturday morning I went up to the quarry firm to get my cards and then I cycled to the NAAFI through the airport. Before you weren't allowed to go there but now you were.

'I wanted to get two packets of cigarettes because they were hard to get elsewhere. I left my bike beside the door of the NAAFI and went in, got my cigarettes and came out and as I was getting my bike straightened out I heard this terrible roar of an aeroplane. The plane hit the NAAFI and burst into flames. A part of the wall came down and knocked me and the bike over. The bike saved me. And the next thing I remember is going along in an ambulance to the Massereene Hospital in Antrim. I thought I was lying in my own bedroom when I was lying in the ambulance.

'My leg and foot must have got a bad knock and they got me into plaster of Paris, I don't mind them X-raying me. I don't think it was ever a job.'

Belgian fish and chips party. (Sourced by François Vincent from the archives of *Banbridge Chronicle*)

10

After the War Was Over

A D-Day was simply a day on which a large military operation was planned. The D-Day remembered by everybody who was living at the time represented the beginning of the end of the war. It was 6 June 1944. Allied forces launched a combined naval, air and land assault on Nazi-occupied France. The event was surrounded by secrecy because the Allies wanted it to be a surprise attack. If you lived in the south of England it was obvious something big was planned because of the build-up of troops and ships in the area. As a result, travel outside the area was strictly forbidden. That caused a lot of heartbreak in ways that were not immediately obvious. My old friend, the late **Edith Chapman,** had at the age of 19 met and married a soldier, **George Chapman**, who had been stationed in Belfast. Shortly after they were married George got a posting in the south of England and the young couple moved to be near his work. Edith told me she was unable to get home when her father was dying because everything was very hush-hush regarding the proposed invasion and it was impossible to leave the area. She deeply regretted not being able to get home to say 'goodbye' to her much-loved father and support her mother. She said, 'My non-appearance caused a lot of friction at the time because some family members thought I didn't want to come home. They didn't believe I simply could not get away.'

William Hillis recounts, 'Before they left for D-Day one of the Americans told my mother they had some bags of coal left and asked if she'd like it. She was delighted because coal was rationed at the time, but she wasn't so pleased when she saw the room where they had lit the fire. They didn't mean any harm but they'd been careless. Americans weren't used to old houses, so they'd allowed red-hot ash from the fire to fall off the hearth and down the gaps between the floorboards on to the joists. There they smouldered and they could have set the whole house on fire.'

Campbell Graham, a family friend, lived on the Stranmillis and attended the Methodist College on the Malone Road. He said, 'You'd have been crazy if you hadn't realised something big was planned. I had to cross the Malone Road to get to school. That was practically impossible because of all the military trucks and tanks driving towards the docks. All the major roads in Belfast were blocked by the military.'

Garnet Chambers remembers the events leading up to D-Day. He says, 'We knew plans were afoot to invade France but the time and place was kept very secret. We had no radio and I remember my father coming in at lunch-time and telling my mother that it was on the news that the invasion had started. A cousin of mine had married a Welsh soldier. He had been on leave a few months earlier and with her had visited us but had not mentioned a thing about it. We did not know at the time if he had even been a part of the invasion. It was some weeks later that we learned he had indeed been a part and that his landing craft had been hit by a shell or a mine and only he and the craft commander had survived. He was badly wounded and was in hospital for some time. He recovered but sadly was killed when his tank hit a landmine during the push to relieve the paratroopers at Arnhem in the autumn. He was a very nice man and I remembered my mother crying and saying "poor Cliff, poor Cliff".'

Eleven months later, on Tuesday, 8 May 1945, VE Day (Victory in Europe) was celebrated. It was the day the Allies accepted Germany's unconditional surrender, thus marking the end of the war in Europe. Derry/Londonderry played such an important part in the Battle of the Atlantic that the quayside at Lisnahally was designated for the surrender of some German U-boats.

Jim (Jimbo) Conway writes, 'My mother told me that after the war ended our returning troops travelled by train, arrived at Lurgan Railway Station and marched through the town. The soldiers had been away from home so long their children could have forgotten what they looked like. An elderly relative recalled as a young boy standing at the railway station each day looking for his returning soldier dad. As the soldiers paraded home they dropped off one by one as they each reached his home. The last to drop off made his way down his street, Brown Street, and he realised this must be his daddy. He ran to him shouting, "Daddy! Daddy! Daddy!"'

George Beattie writes, 'In the final stage of the German defeat they allowed prisoners to escape, so my sister Ruth's fiancé, **Tommy Easton**, managed to make his way back to England.

'Immediately after the war Tommy was repatriated to Australia. Unfortunately he, like his comrades, had to return to Australia by ship and he was forced join them. He managed to get a few days' compassionate leave to marry Ruth, by special licence, in Newry Parish Anglican Church, that is, St Mary's. I remember being there. In those days boys wore short trousers. I'd fallen and cut my knee very badly, so it was covered by a large bandage. My mother suggested I pull what we used to call our stockings (socks) up to hide it, which I did.

'The reception was held in an excellent restaurant overlooking the park in Warrenpoint. The young couple didn't stay very long, so there are no photographs of them. They wanted to make the most of their time together, so caught the train to Portrush for a two-day honeymoon before Tommy had to leave for Australia. Ruth was a war bride and the Australian Navy arranged for her to travel, along with other war brides, on a British aircraft carrier to Australia. She wasn't able to join him for more than two years. It must have been very tough.'

Lisa Rawlins (née Lacey) writes, 'Granda, **Sergeant Jack Lacey,** escaped towards the end of the war when the Germans were losing. There was a great deal of confusion. The Russian Army was advancing and he was helped by a Russian soldier, who managed to get him on a ship sailing to England. Granda arrived safely and was debriefed at an army camp just outside London. He was only there for a few days during which he met up briefly with his family before high-tailing it back to Granny and home as fast as he could go.

'It was a great relief for the family, especially Granny, when Granda eventually returned home. While in Germany he became fluent in the German language. Like many other ex-soldiers he never talked about his wartime experiences. The little I know I picked up from Granny.

'After the war my grandparents set up home in Linenhall Street, Banbridge, and had one child, my mother, Mary Patricia Lacey, known as Pat.

'Granda was resilient. He recovered from his wartime experiences, managed to live a normal life and was well liked and highly thought of around Banbridge. He became an avid Arsenal supporter and worked for many years as a bus driver with the UTA on the Banbridge–Scarva route. Sadly he died of a brain tumour in 1975.'

JR writes, 'We lived on a farm on the outskirts of Sion Mills. British soldiers were billeted in temporary huts above the Prospect Bar, Sion Mills, which gave them a great view of Donegal. We think that this was a resting camp for soldiers to recuperate after the war. This was shortly after the war, around 1945.

'The soldiers walked around the roads to pass the time. On one occasion a soldier came into the byre to watch my father milking a cow.

'Most of the soldiers had never seen a cow being milked and were curious how this was done. We explained the process of hand milking the cows and how the milk was stored until being brought to the creamery.

'This was obviously a new experience to them and they thanked us for letting them watch us at milking.

'When I was going to school one day I met soldiers on the road. One of them gave me chewing gum and told me to just chew it and not to swallow it. This was the first time I had chewing gum.'

The End of Blackout

During the war my mother used to tell me how marvellous it was to be able to see where you were going after dark and not have to bother carrying torches. I loved looking at the stars and was very disappointed when the street lights came on and I couldn't see them. The street had lights that were powered by gas. We had a lamp lighter called **Derek McBride**, who lit the lamps manually at dusk and turned them off when the sun came up. He was very friendly and children where I lived enjoyed chatting to him. He rode between lamp posts on a bicycle, climbed up on the lamp posts and dealt with each individual lamp. He was very pleasant and always had a cheery word.

Petrol Rationing Ends

Petrol rationing ended in May 1951 and after that it became possible to travel, wherever you wanted, by car. People preferred to do their own shopping rather than rely on street traders and they slowly declined and eventually disappeared.

Anne Henry (née Finlay) beside the family car. (Photograph by Bill Henry)

Jay remembers the day her family car 'was brought back into the daylight.' Its tyres had perished completely and the wheels sat sadly on the flattened tyres. Still, the local mechanic lived nearby, surviving on his second skill as a blacksmith, and cars were soon on the road again.

Heather Taylor's description of life immediately after the war shows that there were few changes in lifestyle. Heather writes, 'I was born in the Old Hospital, Banbridge, on 10 March 1944 and went to live with my grandparents at 1 Prospect Terrace because my father was in Europe fighting in the war. He chose my name and I was christened Heather Lynda Hayes in Seapatrick Parish Church.

'My great-grandfather lived with us. I remember he always wore a flat cap. I can't ever remember him talking it off, although I've been told if anyone ever raised their voice at me he threw it at them and never missed!

'At that time Prospect Park was surrounded by open land with a hockey field, surrounded by a green corrugated fence in front. There were crab apple trees in the hockey field and Nana and I used to pick windfalls and make jam. I remember the glorious smells that wafted around the kitchen. Dad played hockey and Banbridge was proud of its hockey team. It brought back a trophy from Eire and had something to celebrate.

'There were no mod cons. Everything was done by hand. You had a time for doing each household chore. Grandmother got up at 6 a.m. every morning to clean and polish the range for the day ahead, light the fire and prepare breakfast.

'Before going to work (in the linen industry) Grandad made sure there was enough wood and coal to keep the fire alight during the day. He brought down and emptied the chamber pot (if used) in the toilet, which was outside. It was all right on a dry day but wasn't so funny when it rained! Then there was the question of toilet paper! It was made from yesterday's newspaper cut into squares and hung on a nail on the wall. We did have a nice toilet roll, but it was kept for visitors and it was back to the newspaper as soon as they left.

'My aunt and uncle lived in Kenlis Street. I loved visiting them and was fascinated by Uncle's dahlias. Some of the blooms were so large I could hide behind them.

'Granda went walking every evening with his friends come rain, hail or snow. One evening the sky turned black and there was a thunderstorm. We were scared and raced up the stairs to hide under the bed. As we passed a window a very bright bolt of lightning hit a large tree in the hockey field and set it alight. We were very relieved when Granda arrived safely home.

'Every Sunday afternoon we walked miles along the Castlewellan Road. I filled my favourite basket from the sea of yellow primroses in the hedgerows and made posies to give to Nana's neighbours.

'My parents moved from Banbridge when I was 4 but I spent all the time I could with Nana and Granda. I now have come full circle, returned to Banbridge and live in house built on the hills I used to walk with Grandad.'

Availability of Goods

Proper toilet paper became available after the war. It was thin, more like tracing paper than the soft paper we know and love today. If you wrapped a single piece around a comb, put your lips against it and hummed, it sounded like a mouth organ and Colin, a friend, says he used it as tracing paper.

Not everybody could afford toilet paper, as Heather writes (see above), so many people stuck to squares of newspapers, unless they expected visitors. There's an old story I'm sure's true about a wee lad who returned a roll of toilet paper to his local corner shop and said to the shopkeeper, 'Me Ma says, please would you exchange this for a packet of Woodbine. Our visitors didn't come!'

Housing

Thanks to the Blitz there was a severe housing shortage when people returned home after the war. In 1945 the government started building pre-fabs to increase the housing stock. They went up very quickly and their owners thought they were wonderful! They had all mod cons, including fridges! They were considered a temporary solution to an acute problem but unfortunately they were made of asbestos. The link between asbestos and diseases of the lungs, including cancer, was unknown. Several schools were built of asbestos, including Ashfield Girls Secondary Intermediate School and Ashfield Boys Secondary Intermediate School in Belfast.

Once, on holiday I visited Exeter Cathedral and had a guided tour by a wonderful old gentleman who had served in the Army during the war. He said, 'After the war I was sent to the Army camp in Holywood, County Down. It was in a terrible state. Poor lads and lasses came back after serving their country and had nowhere to go so they squatted in the old Army Nissen huts. The Army had destroyed all the sanitary facilities, so the poor souls did what they had to do between the huts. It was disgusting. We had to clean it up after they left.'

Today the site is known as the Palace Barracks, Holywood. It is still used by the Army.

On the other hand, many people would have been happy to get their homes back! **George Nesbitt** writes, 'My home was overcrowded during the war because two refugee ladies were billeted in our dining room and two more in the living room. These ladies fended for themselves, cooking over an open fire. They worked locally in the office of Walkers factory. We also had a cousin, his wife and two children living with us during the war. In total we had thirteen people living in the house. Five Nesbitts, four cousins and four refugees. It was nice to have the place to ourselves again!'

George Beattie as a young man. (Printed with kind permission of George Beattie)

Regeneration

Regeneration of housing stock began after the war with the aim of supplying everyone with proper living and toilet facilities. This was done with the best of intentions but had the effect of breaking up communities and causing future trouble.

The late **Seamus Lavery** describes in his poem 'My Wee House' what his mother felt. Hers was a typical reaction:

> A lock of months back, this letter did come,
> Which said my wee house was only a slum,
> My lovely wee house, that knowed sweet times and bitter,
> Was now called a slum by a City Hall skitter.
>
> Well I nearly dropped dead where I stood on the floor,
> When in comes wee Cissie, m'neighbour next due,
> The colour of death, and I wasn't much better,
> And she held in her hand, the very same letter.

Of course, the people protested, to no avail. They were rehoused and Seamus used his mother's feelings to describe what happened next:

> When I redd out m'wee house, m'heart was real sore,
> And I thought m'wee house sensed, I'd be back no more,
> For the door gave a screech, and the windies all shook,
> As I stud on the footpath, t'have my last look.
>
> Well they put him an' me in a high rise flat,
> With people on this side and people on that,
> With people above us and people below,
> But not one friendly face in that place did I know
> In my own wee house I could always luk out,

And see wee children all playing' about,
An take m'wee stool, and sit at the door,
But in this wee flat I cud just see the sky and the floor.

Seamus told me he was inspired to write 'My Wee House' when he met his mother on the street and she was crying. She had just seen the end of her dear old home:

Then one day last week I went for a dander,
As they say where the heart lies, the feet always wander,
I walked to the street where I'd lived all my life,
First as a child and then as a wife.

When I saw my wee house, I just stud there and cried,
I felt cold all over, and empty inside,
My house, that had sheltered my family and me,
Was stripped bare and naked, for all eyes to see

Then down the street came this big crane,
With a big iron ball on a long heavy chain,
It stopped just fernenst* me, and then swung round,
And my poor wee house was brought to the ground.

I opened my mouth, but I just couldn't spake,
I had the same feeling ye get at a wake,
A lifetime of caring had just come to an end,
And I'd just seen the end of a very dear friend.

I turned on m'heel, and m'legs were shaking,
I walked slowly away, with a heart that was breakin'
I went towards that flat, with a feelin' of dread,
And I wished like my wee house, I wished I was dead.

*next to

Redevelopment destroyed the old communities along with the old community spirit.

'Wee' houses in inner-city Belfast.

Travel

George Beattie records, 'In the 1950s Dundalk Cycling Club went on a cycling trip to Scotland. They cycled to Belfast and took the ferry over to Scotland. Most members had small tricolours attached to their bikes. On their return journey the riders were detained by the RUC because displaying tricolours was illegal at the time.

'Air travel was either non-existent or very expensive until the early 1960s. Until the time of partition in 1921 the fastest way to travel from Belfast to London was on the express steam train that operated from Belfast's Great Victoria Street Railway Station. It was a beautiful building, completed in 1848 and described by John Betjeman as "one of the finest examples of Victorian Railway Stations". During the early 1980s Great Victoria Street was bombed by the IRA on several occasions, causing extensive damage that ultimately led to the demolition of the 1848 terminus building.

'Living in Greenore, as I did as a child, I became fascinated by trains and boats. When I took my wife, **Elizabeth**, to England we went across to Glas–

gow from Belfast on the ferry. I was extravagant. I hired a cabin, which was much better than bunking down on the deck as I had done previously when I went on camping holidays across the water. Ferries were very different from those sailing today. There were two classes, third class and saloon class, which were separated by iron gates. The bars in the gates were rather like those of the cages of animals in the zoo. Third-class passengers used to crowd together to look at those on the far side, so I'm not sure who was the monkey! Saloon passengers appeared to have plenty of room, while we were packed like sardines.

'Cabins on the ferries were basic, but adequate. Our two-berth cabin had two bunk beds, one above the other. There was a tiny wash-hand basin and a toilet in a cubicle facing the door. In the morning a steward brought you a couple of slices of burnt toast and a cup of tea that was so strong it cut the tartar off your teeth, but it was very welcome. Basic as it was, it was much better than sleeping in one of the dormitories or on deck!'

Local residents who hopped on the train from Dromore to Hillsborough on 29 April 1956 can still recall that journey to this day because this was the last time it operated on that line. **Bob Beggs** was only 3 at the time. He recounts, 'My late dad **Robbie** and sister **May** made the journey to give the train a befitting send-off. They realised the historic importance of the occasion, so kept their train tickets as mementoes.

Tickets for the last train from Banbridge.
(printed with kind permission of Bob Beggs)

'Dad sadly passed on in 1995 but his sister May Beggs remembers to this day what was effectively the end of an era. She was a few days short of her 13th birthday at the time. As it was the "end of the line" for Hillsborough train station there was no return service available, however Dad and May were able to get a lift from Mother's uncle, who had a car.'

By mid-1955, in keeping with the wider trend, road transport was fast taking over from rail links, but no matter how popular buses and cars had become, the closure of Hillsborough train station was heartbreaking, bearing in mind that it had been in existence since 1863. It was part of the Great Northern Railway (Ireland) system. The station closed the day after that last train ride under the auspices of the Great Northern Railway Board. Train services were replaced by buses provided by the Ulster Transport Authority (UTA). The station was removed when the dual carriageway was built. It was situated where the A1 crosses over the Culcavey Road and the Dromore train station is the Old Station Nursery School.

Joe Furphy was on that last train. He recalled: 'For the first time I was able to travel first class! I paid the sum of 3s 6d from Banbridge to Dromore! By travelling first class I was able to enjoy a forward view, sitting in the front compartment of the three-coach diesel. I kept my ticket! In the same compartment to me on that train was an "Inst" boy, Lindsay Taggart, whom I got to know at Queen's University. It was only then that we found out over a cup of coffee in the students' union that we had been on that train! Being both passionate about all things railway-related, he and I visited the signal cabins at Great Victoria Street – legally – and in Lisburn – unofficially! We also visited Maysfield yard when it held a large number of locomotives destined for scrap.'

Changes in Diet

Before and during the war a typical main meal consisted of potatoes, meat and a vegetable, followed by a sweet, such as bread and butter pudding, rice pudding, stewed apple and custard or strawberries, when they were in season. The introduction of package holidays after the war led to the demand for what we thought of as 'foreign' food. I remember my family on holiday in Dublin thinking we were the height of sophistication dining on chicken Maryland (deep-fat-fried breaded chicken, fried apple, banana and bacon) served with mashed and roast potatoes. Eating spaghetti and macaroni felt like an adventure. The first Chinese restaurant, The Peacock, opened during the early 1960s in Belfast. We watched cooking programmes in darkened rooms on black-and-white television sets with presenters such as Philip Harben and Fanny Cradock (known locally as Fanny Haddock).

A Fine Romance

Bridgeen Rutherford describes the result of the romance between her aunt, **Maureen Woods**, and American soldier **Mel Woods**. 'After D-Day Mel was sent to France to complete more duties and then returned to the US. Maureen was an avid letter writer and spent some time writing to Mel's mother in the States. Mel never put pen to paper. He just showed up at the bar unexpectedly and was made very welcome.

'Maureen and Mel were married on 5 November 1946 in the Waterside Chapel by **Fr O'Hagan** with Maureen's cousin, **Patsy Elliott** and her younger sister **Ethna Elliott** as their respective best man and bridesmaid. The happy couple headed to Dublin for their honeymoon. Maureen was not a "war bride" but Mel and his Derry bride met during wartime. The *Derry Journal* dated Wednesday, 6 November 1946 carried the story of their wedding along with two photographs, one of the bridal party and the other showing off their three-tier cake at their wedding reception in the old City Hotel in Derry.

'They settled in Sag Harbor, Long Island, raising their family of five children. Mel died in May 1972 and Maureen died in July 2001. She had several visits back home to Derry during her lifetime. One of her brothers followed her to the US and some of her sisters also managed to visit and spend some time with Maureen while she was living in Sag Harbor.

'At one visit to my own home she happened to mention that one of her names was Philomena, as is one of mine. I was delighted to find this out as I had always wondered where my mother had plucked this name from. Maureen was a very special aunt with whom I shared letters and I have retained some in my prized possessions.'

Norman and Elizabeth Finlay's wedding in 1946 before the end of clothes rationing. (Printed with kind permission of Vernon Finlay)

Wedding of Jeannie and Wilbert McMaster in 1953. Jeannie is wearing a fashionable wedding dress influenced by 'Dior's New Look' with a flared skirt that used a lot of material following the end of clothes rationing in 1949. (Printed with kind permission of Anne McMaster)

JJ and Susan got married in the '60s long after clothes rationing, so Susan's wedding dress is no longer restricted by shortages and resembles those worn today. (Printed with kind permission of JJ Woods)

Life on a Smallholding After the War

Florence Chambers (née Dickson) records, 'My parents married late in life so Mum was 42 when I was born, in Banbridge Hospital at the end of January in 1947. That was the year of "the big snow", so Mum and I were marooned in hospital until well into February. Mum was churning butter when her waters broke and Father managed to get her to Banbridge Hospital, as a semi-private patient. It started to snow, he had difficulty getting home and didn't get to see me for several days. Aunt Florrie came to the rescue at the weekend. She worked in Belfast and managed to get a train to Banbridge and walked from the station to Banbridge Hospital, bringing much-needed supplies such as baby clothes.

'I lived on a 6-acre farm, in a house called Hillrest, on Leapogues Road in the townland of Drumiller between Dromara and Dromore with my mother, father and Aunt Florrie, who lived in Belfast, but spent weekends at our home. Father was the headmaster of Skeagh Primary School. When he was appointed, the school management committee wanted to build him a school house, as was the practice in those days. Father was a very independent man so he refused the offer and bought Hillrest. It was about 3 miles from the school, so during the war, as he had a bad heart, he was given a petrol allowance to enable him to get to work.

'As a child I had everything I could want except a sibling. I was kept for months in a large pram at the far end of our lawn, away from trouble. I remember crawling out of the pram and creeping in through our front door and finding my mother's wooden spool box. I had great fun crawling around all the furniture in the drawing room with different-coloured spools. Thread everywhere! Our neighbour, **Mrs Sudlow**, was in the house chatting with Mum. Eventually they heard the rattling in the hall and emerged to find me, by now hiding round the back of a chair. Laughter was followed by the horror of trying to unravel all my good work.

'I remember a very needy young mother, with a couple of children, coming, on foot, to our house and my pram, early clothing being sold to them. I wasn't encouraged to play with any other children. There weren't any until two years after I was born. The next house was an off-licence premises about 400 yards away, and the family had two children, a girl and a boy. I only met them years later when going to the local Sunday School.

'There were wonderful fireplaces in the main bedrooms of our house and I remember being washed and dressed in front of a warm fire while frost flowers glistened on the single-glazed windows in the wintertime. We had a flush toilet in an outhouse at the bottom of our farmyard. The water for flushing was obtained from the guttering around a number of attached out-houses. What we called our "rough water" came from a huge tank inside the house that collected water from the roof. It was not connected to a public supply of water and it was unusual for a house in the country to have a sitter supply for such things as baths. We had good lighting run from Calor gas cylinders under the stairs with piped gas supplying the rooms. It wasn't the kind of installation that would have been approved by Health and Safety but it did the job. We paid for the installation of electricity in November 1955. Father was very modern in his outlook and he bought Mum a vacuum cleaner so we had one in anticipation of having electricity.

'Mum had a large vegetable garden. She grew potatoes, carrots, turnips, peas, beans, cauliflowers, every vegetable you could think of along with black, red and white currants and strawberries. That fed us as and we shared with friends in Belfast. Food was rationed until early 1950s but as we also had chickens, eggs and cows for milk there was really no shortage for us.

'Mum bred turkeys for the Christmas trade. I hated plucking them, which started in early December. The outhouse was cold and we stood on a con-crete floor with a huge wooden box for the feathers. Sometimes we had to clean out the innards, which was always a stinking nasty job. The birds were strung up on hooks for a couple of weeks and then the customers would arrive for their bird. The cold floors gave us chilblains on our feet. They caused scars on poor Mum's feet. They felt itchy and sore, so she used to give them ease by walking, with bare feet, in snow. I know the old folklore for chilblains is to put your feet in a urine-filled biscuit box. We never did that!'

Shopping

Florence Chambers continues: 'After the war it was a routine for Mum and Aunt Florrie to go into Dromore on a Saturday evening, in the car, to do some shopping and meet friends. Shops opened until 9 p.m. in those days. When very young I was left at home tucked up in bed with my father babysitting. We parked the car, took our shopping basket and entered a shop, bought whatever we wanted, then walked to the next shop and bought whatever you wanted, then went to the next shop and so on. There were no supermarkets and the shops were very different from those today. Butcher's shops had floors covered in sawdust to soak up possible blood spillages that

Shop in Ballyclare in 1947. (Printed with kind permission of Vernon Finlay)

could have leaked from the skinned carcasses hanging suspended by their hind legs on hooks at the top of the wall behind the counter. Some butcher's shops had carcasses hanging outside the shop. They attracted flies that laid eggs which hatched into maggots, and it was the butcher boy's job to sweep them off every morning. The display under the glass counter top looked much as it does today.

'We shopped in **Paddy Neeson**'s store in Dromore. **Alice Neeson** was in the office, but **Pat Rooney** and a fellow called **Burns** were the shop boys. I particularly loved a pink sweet – hazelnut creams. They had rose-flavoured fondant and cost 10 pence a quarter in the early '50s, just as rationing lifted.

'I loved going into Dale's Chemist Shop in Dromore as there was a large fish tank, it was wonderful to see the coloured fish and the large carboys filled with different-coloured water. **Mr MacLaine** was a lovely assistant, who liked to hear me singing. After the Dales retired and **Norman Weir** took over, **Mrs Hannah Weir** and he were both qualified pharmacists and coped without Mr MacLaine. He got another job in Alexander Boyd's Pharmacy in Lisburn, so we used to visit him there.

'I loved going to Belfast to see Santa Claus in either Robbs or the Co-op. Driving up and down the main streets with all the lights on and windows dressed for Christmas. I thought that was magical as our country roads were always dark.

'Folks from Belfast loved to come to the country at the weekends to get away from the smoke and smog. I suppose that started during the war years. We got friendly with many of those who rented cottages. It was my job to deliver milk and eggs to one lady in particular, **May Kerr**. She in turn was able to get beautiful linen tablecloths for Mum from her workplace, Ulster Weavers. They travelled by bus to Dromore and a taxi for the last 3 miles.'

Heather Taylor recalls shopping in Banbridge after the war. She writes, 'I loved going shopping with Nana. Banbridge was magical to me. I said hello to people and they gave me money for ice cream.

'The first person we visited was **Mr Crozier**, the butcher, who made great sausages. I can taste them now.

'I loved Andrew's shop and its high counters with curved glass on top so you could see broken biscuits. I was amazed by how they weighed out sugar and tea, put it into bags and sealed them by just folding them. I loved Woolworth and Woolco, but the highlight of the shopping trip was a visit to Fusco Ice Cream Parlour, where I enjoyed sitting in the booths.'

Clothes Rationing Ends in 1949

Patsy Quinn, who spent the war in Newry says, 'After the war there must have been a lot of material for making the uniforms left over and the cloth was made into boys' trousers. The brother and I were taken to a shop that later became Woolworths (one of our neighbours called it Woolworks) and we got two pairs of really nice short trousers.'

Jim Taylor writes, 'I was born on 10 May 1945, at home in 165 Conway Street off the Shankill Road Belfast, two days after Victory in Europe Day. I feel I was lucky because I missed the war but the bad news was I was a sickly child. Everything I ate or drank came out both ends as liquid.

'The doctors told my parents that there was nothing they could do for me and they should prepare for the worst. Mr Orr, the minister from Conway Street Mission, called in to see me and told my parents that if the worst should happen he would arrange my funeral service.

'Good luck intervened because my mum, May Taylor, heard about a chemist on the Hollywood Road who was mixing his own medicine and that he might be able to help.

'Mum and her sister Betty walked about 4 miles from the Shankill to the Hollywood Road to save money on trams or buses. They needed all the money they had to purchase the medicine.

'They told the chemist about my sickness. He made up two bottles of medicine but they only had enough money to pay for one and a half bottles. The kindly chemist took the money for one bottle and gave them the other free. He told them to use the little money they had left to get bus or tram home. Three weeks after starting the medicine I improved rapidly. The doctor was impressed!

'Four years after I was born, my dad, **Albert Taylor**, and his brothers, **Kenny Taylor** and **Jim Taylor**, were going to Manchester to see a football match on the Friday, 19 August 1949. They set off in Kenny's 1934 Austin 7 to Nutts Corner Airport to catch the British European Airways 10 a.m. flight to Manchester, on a Douglas Dakota airplane. (Aldergrove International Airport replaced Nutts Corner as Belfast's main airport when it was opened by Elizabeth, The Queen Mother on 28 October 1963. Previously it had been used by the RAF.) On the way to the airport the car broke down. They tried to get a taxi (mobile phones hadn't been invented) but they had to walk miles to reach a phone box. They eventually got to the airport ten minutes after take-off. They called Kenny everything! Later in the Glenco Bar, opposite my grandmother's house, they heard that the plane had crashed on Saddleworth Moor, 15 miles from Manchester Airport. Twenty-one of the twenty-nine passengers and all the crew died, leaving just eight survivors. Uncle Kenny was forgiven and probably didn't need to buy any drinks the rest of the night!

'I was lucky I wasn't affected by the tragedy of the bomb on Percy Street and the terrible air crash, but I really feel for all those who lost their lives.'

The Showband Era

The advent of the car gave rise to the showband era with its ritual of young people dressing up when they went to dances, either with a partner or with the intention of 'clicking'.

The showbands grew out of the big bands, such as **Billy Cotton's Big Band**, which broadcast frequently on BBC radio. They had a least ten musicians with saxophones, trumpets, trombones and a rhythm section. The musicians were formally dressed, with formal suits and bow ties, and they usually provided easy listening music at formal events.

Showbands were smaller, informal and the musicians dressed in lightweight suits. There were more than 500 showbands playing in ballrooms, marquees and dance halls in the late '50s. Top bands included **Clipper Carlton** from Strabane, **The Melody Aces** from Newtownstewart, **Johnny Quigley Allstars** and **Gay McIntyre's Band** from Derry/Londonderry and **Dave Glover's Showband** from Newtownabbey. Apart from the top bands, there were dozens

Larry Breen as a young man. (Printed with kind permission of Larry Breen)

of others working just as hard throughout Ireland. Every sizeable town had its own dance hall, and what better place for boy meets girl? Rock and roll was the order of the day.

The Banbridge's Castle Ballroom, like other ballrooms throughout Ireland, was a cauldron of excitement, energy, fun and enjoyment for many young people, but it was much more than that. It was where many people met, formed lasting relationships, married and settled down – and unfortunately it caused a few broken hearts as well. They were truly 'Ballrooms of Romance'.

Larry Breen describes a typical night out. He writes, 'Although born and living in Lurgan, I would have frequented ballrooms from as near as my home town Lurgan to as far away as Derry. The Castle in Banbridge was very popular, a great night out and comparable to any ballroom I danced in, and sure remember, "that dear little town in the auld County Down was full of beautiful girls". I remember some memorable nights there dancing the night away.'

The Saturday night ritual in the Castle Ballroom was also acted out in every ballroom in the country and it tells a unique story of entertainment and a way of life now only a distant memory.

Larry goes on to describe how getting 'dolled up' was important with a wash and a shave, and I myself remember well that Brylcreem and Old Spice were the order of the day. There was no alcohol at the dance, the dancing was from 9–1 or 10–2, so we would drop into the Coach Inn for a few drinks before the dance, always helped with some 'Dutch courage'.

Girls also dressed up, making sure they were 'right up the oxyters' (armpits), with carefully applied make-up, mascara, eyeshadow, lipstick, wearing their best dress, or a skirt and blouse with a tiny waist, and shoes with high heels! Trainers had not yet developed out of gym shoes. In England they were called plimsoles. In Ireland we referred to them as 'gutties' or 'mutton dummies'! I, being small, always trotted around wearing 6in high heels in an attempt to make myself taller! In common with other young women, I could walk confidently in them without wobbling the way young woman do today because they aren't accustomed to them.

Larry says, 'The scene on the dance floor was a sight to behold; girls on one side and boys on the opposite side. It reminded me of my primary school days when we were separated, boys and girls, by a line in the playground that you could not cross. However, crossing the ballroom floor was paramount if you were to have any chance of meeting a potential sweetheart. We were like athletes ready for the gun to sound and then it was a charge to get to the best-looking girls on the other side. It could be a blow to your self-esteem if you were refused but normally with the large numbers milling around it was not too obvious.

'The music was exceptional, much better than today, with high-quality bands capable of playing all the music and songs of the day. The sound of the Twist, the Hucklebuck and Lonnie Donegan's skiffle music still ring in my ears. There was no limit to our repertoire: slow waltz, old-time waltz, foxtrot and, of course, jiving and be-bopping. It was difficult to talk to your partner during dances except for a slow waltz when there was an opportunity to get a bit more up close and personal.

'There was always one ladies' choice and this was great because it could be a signal that you were possibly on for "getting off your mark". There was no alcohol available but you could ask a girl up for a soft drink accompanied by crisps or peanuts. This was the opportunity to go for the kill and ask her out, hopefully for a "wee court".

'The main object of the night was to "get off your mark" and have a "wee court". Sometimes there would be four of us travelling in the one car, which presented some problems with regard to "courting". Two lucky ones would get the front and back seat of the car and the other two unlucky ones would have to be content with a suitable gateway. Often the "wee court" would lead to a date at the picture house the following week, maybe the Iveagh in Banbridge or the Lyric in Lurgan.'

Margaret Jones was born in Banbridge and didn't have the advantage of owning a car, so she had to travel by foot and trip the light fantastic in her hometown. As a teenager she looked forward to Saturday nights when she went to the dance held in the Castle Ballroom, Banbridge, which was regarded locally as the place to go. Margaret says, 'It attracted people from all arts and parts and the bands were fantastic. **Ruby Murray** often came and sang there. Imagine that! A wee girl from Benburb Street in South Belfast who had number one hits in the charts in both America and in the UK sang in the Castle Ballroom in Banbridge! I was allowed to go there with my cousin, **Renee Gamble**, because it was reckoned to be a respectable place, unlike the Orange Hall where fights sometimes broke out.

'I never learned to dance but in its heyday the Castle ballroom floor was crowded, so all I had to do was shuffle around in time to the music and I could do that! I had to leave before the dance ended because my mother insisted I was home before midnight because the next day was the Sabbath day. I used to stay until the last moment and run like the wind to be at home on time, or I was in trouble.

'Most people dressed up in their Sunday best and went to church. Girls and women wore hats and gloves, while the men were clothed in dark suits with a shirt and tie. Casual dress was frowned upon. On Sundays everywhere, apart from the churches, was shut. No pubs, no picture houses, no shops or play parks and you couldn't sit on a swing or drop into a wee cafe for a cuppa because they were closed. Some people took it to extremes and wouldn't even clean their shoes or watch television after it became a common possession in the early '60s. Mother took the Sabbath day very seriously, so just before midnight she stood outside our front door giving out! "It's the Sabbath day. Hurry up! Hurry up! It's time you were in!"

'Renee and I went to the Castle ballroom for the craic and because we wanted to get boyfriends. We'd line up on the girls' side of the room, hopefully eyeing the talent and deciding who we'd ask for the eagerly awaited "ladies' choice". When it was announced, the stampede across the floor was like the charge of the Light Brigade. If you fancied a particularly good-looking fella you had to be quick to reach him before he was lifted by somebody else!'

During the war, clothes were made in as economical a way as possible. In 1947 Dior introduced what was known as 'the new look', designing women's clothes with voluminous skirts. The way was paved for wide skirts once clothes rationing ended in 1949. Margaret records, 'Renee and I felt the quare goat's toes as we paraded into the ballroom with our voluminous petticoats hidden under our full skirts with their tight waists. Elastic belts were fashionable and I had one I loved. We loved our poppet beads! You could buy them in places like Woolworths. They were dirt cheap, made of plastic. You could pull them apart or join long chains together, and you had earrings to match.

'We sat on the chairs placed in a row along the sides of the dance floor, which had a lovely springy feel. Sometimes there were a few couples dancing before the night got properly under way. One couple particularly caught my eye. I didn't know who they were at the time, but years later I was introduced to them, **Nan McCall** and **Andy White**. Nan lived on a farm at Collon, near Markethill, and had met Andy at a dance in the Portadown's

Seagoe. They got married and came to live on Andy's family farm near Ban-bridge. They were excellent dancers who looked very elegant as they twirled around the floor with Nan's skirts swirling as they turned. Eventually they were joined by others and the hall grew more and more crowded and hotter and hotter, fuelled by the excitement rising from sweating bodies until con-densation rained from the low ceiling onto our heads and shoulders.

'There was a wee kiosk beside the place you bought your entrance ticket. It sold, among other things, Wagon Wheels and a fizzy drink called Vimto. We bought and devoured with relish during the interval. In retrospect I can't think of anything more revolting!

'One night Renee clicked! A fella asked her to meet him inside the Orange Hall the following Saturday. She really fancied him, so we decided to risk it and set out the following Saturday night for the Orange Hall. It was very disappointing. He didn't turn up and worse was to follow. It began to rain and I'd come out without my raincoat. My mother decided to bring it to the Castle ballroom. Of course, I wasn't there! My friends told her I'd gone to the Orange Hall and when I came out she was standing at the door with a face like a Lurgan spade! I'm telling you she sang up and down the scale and gave me the Ten Commandments, the Lord's Prayer, the lot, the whole way home ! I had to promise, on my word of honour, I'd never go to the Orange Hall again! I never did.'

George Nesbitt says, 'I learnt to drive when my father bought a Vauxhall car. I'd been driving for a long time before I was allowed to take it out at night and I could find entertainment further afield. One night I met my fate when I went to a dance in Portadown and saw Sadie Grant. I thought she was wonderful and eventually we got married. She died of cancer thirteen years ago and I still think she was wonderful.'

An old friend, the late **Billy Simpson**, who grew up in Portrush, told me how much he enjoyed going to what he described as 'the hop' each Saturday night in the Arcadia Ballroom. He said, 'During the summer months train-loads of holidaymakers used to arrive in Portrush Railway Station.'

Billy and the boys made sure they got a good position across the road, 'We were breathing vitality and lush, and probably cigarette smoke, and as we tried to look cool and eyed the talent. To a man we ended up in the Arcadia that night. Unfortunately we couldn't afford the entrance, so we pooled our pennies and bought one ticket. The one with the ticket walked in legally, flashing his ticket, and went straights to the gents, went into one of the cubicles, shut the door firmly and opened the window. The other boys climbed up the cliff, got onto the windowsill and in through the window. It was very difficult manoeuvring in through a small upper window and into the building without falling down the loo! It was worth it! It was fantastic, and if you clicked and were allowed to see a girl back to her B&B you were landed! You just had to be careful not to ask a girl to dance before the interval because you'd be expected to buy her a soft drink. There was no alcohol.'

Unfortunately in 1950 Banbridge had cause to remember one of the worst aspects of the Second World War when a plane crashed into Bally-money Hill. **Margaret Graham** says, 'I'll never forget the Sunday afternoon when half the town, dressed in their Sunday best, was walking up the town when we heard a plane in obvious distress. Ballymoney Hill wasn't built up the way it is now, so we could see what was happening. The plane was obviously going to crash and was headed straight for the top of the hill and Mackey's farmhouse. Thankfully it missed the house and hit the hill. The plane blew up, shattering the windows of the old farmhouse, which was badly damaged. The Mackeys rushed to help the pilot. He'd been killed.'

The late **Mrs Mackey** told me, in the late 1970s, of the terror she and her family felt when they saw a plane belching smoke and heading towards their farmhouse at the top of Ballymoney. She said, 'We didn't know where to go! It was heading for us, but where was it going to land? We stood there, mesmerised.' She said she found an engagement ring, which she was able to return to the pilot's fiancée.

François Vincent found a report on the crash in the *Banbridge Chronicle*'s archives. It read as follows:

A fatal aeroplane accident occurred in Banbridge last Sunday afternoon when a single seater Spitfire attached to 502 Ulster Squadron, RAF, crashed in a field about 30 yards from the home of Mr Stanley Mackey, Ballymoney Hill.

About 4.30pm, planes were heard circling around. The afternoon was cloudy with occasional showers and several people who were about at the time saw a plane diving earthward at lightning speed.

Within a few minutes, there was a terrific explosion followed by a flash of flames and huge volumes of smoke.

The force with which the plane struck the ground was shown by the large cavity and the depth to which it buried itself.

The wreckage was strewn over a wide area and pieces of the fuselage lodged in trees in the immediate vicinity.

The effects of the explosion were felt at houses in other parts of the town.

The Spitfire continued to blaze furiously and the Fire Service was summoned and was quickly at the scene.

The flames having been extinguished, the grim work of digging into the wreckage began.

Eventually the remains of the pilot were recovered and conveyed to the morgue at Banbridge Hospital.

In the meantime, a body of RAF men arrived from Aldergrove and there was a most impressive moment when they stood to salute, as the ambulance was moving off.

It transpired that the victim of the crash was Pilot II Ronald Gant, a 27-year-old school teacher, who resided at Mount Charles, Belfast.

Mr Gant joined the RAF in 1940 and became a warrant officer staff pilot.

He was demobbed in 1946 and entered Larkfield Training College, where he qualified as a teacher.

He was on the teaching staff at Gilnahirk Primary School and was interred in the graveyard of Drumbeat Parish Church.

Making Music

People from Northern Ireland tend to be musical and as a result local amateur musical societies, music groups, bands and so on thrived before, during and after the Second World War and were well supported.

Banbridge Choral Society was founded in 1943. At first it produced serious works, such as Handel's *Messiah*, and members dressed in traditional style with the men in dress suits and bow ties while the women wore long black skirts and white blouses. Shortly after the war they decided to indulge in musical theatre.

Margaret Jones says, 'Sometimes the length of time it took to rehearse a show led to difficulties. I remember auditioning for, and getting, the part of one of the three little maids from school in *The Mikado*. I became pregnant shortly afterwards and grew progressively less like a little maid during rehearsals. During the live performance I had difficulty bending over in the way the part demanded!

'The Choral Society didn't have a lot of money. We existed hand to mouth and couldn't afford hire costumes, so we made our own. That was difficult with clothes rationing and shortages of materials. During the dress rehearsal of *Iolanthe* the producer said the fairies needed a bit more glitter. We put our heads together and decided the best thing we could do was sew milk bottle tops around the hems of our white fairy dresses. (In those days bottles of milk were delivered to household doors and each bottle had a tinfoil cap.) We were really pleased with our efforts until we started to dance and realised our bits of glitter knocked together and clanked. Later a member of the audience told us he'd never seen so many pregnant-looking fairies. The singing was of a very high standard, although the sets and costumes were awful. But sure it was all good clean fun.'

Alan Burns says, 'I got a big part in *The Belle of New York*. Me and two other men had a complicated routine with figures of eights in it. We were really nervous, praying we wouldn't make a mistake and bump into each other on stage. We were pleased with our performance. We didn't make any mistakes but felt puzzled because of the audience reaction. It was quite a serious piece and everyone was laughing. We'd a quick change in the wings before going on. When we came off stage we were told we'd forgotten to do up our spares! What an embarrassment! We'd been so busy concentrating on our steps we hadn't heard the prompts!'

Local audiences love it when things go wrong! I remember being at a comparatively recent local performance by the amateur South Down Orchestra when the harpist broke a string. A loud 'ping' resounded through the hall and a loud voice from the back shouted, 'Hey Missus! Yer stay's broke.' The place erupted with laughter, including the unfortunate orchestra. The lead double bass dropped his instrument and mayhem ensued. The conductor was forced to stop the performance and restart, but we all had a great time. Good music and a bit of fun, what more could you ask? It was available before, during and after the war.

The Advent of Television

Television wasn't available before, during and immediately after the war. A TV was a huge box in those days with a receiver housed behind a small screen with a small, fuzzy black-and-white picture that had to be viewed in a darkened room. Whole families used to line up in happy anticipation as they watched the screen saver while waiting for the programmes to begin. The night's entertainment ended when an orchestra played the national anthem. Several people have said that their elderly relatives insisted the minute they heard the first note of 'God Save the Queen' they should stand to attention and show respect. There was only one programme, BBC One. It started at 6 p.m. and ended at 10 p.m.. Many families bought a TV in 1953 because they wanted to watch the coronation of Queen Elizabeth II. My parents didn't buy a television until 1954. Family friends **Tom and Eileen Crocker** lived on the Castlereagh Road and it was a big treat to be invited round to their house, where we saw such programmes as the *Television Toppers*, dancing girls with long legs and bowler hats, as well as some programmes that today would not be considered politically correct, such as *The Black and White Minstrel Show*. Never has sitting in a darkened room been so exciting!

Shops in The Square, Dromore County Down. (Printed with kind permission of Florence Chambers)

Belfast was the first place in Northern Ireland to have television, while Dromore in County Down was the second. After months of determined experimenting with various aerials and different locations, P.E. Neeson succeeded in obtaining a reasonably good picture on a television receiver and the local press stated, 'It is hoped that when a "TV" station is erected in Northern Ireland it will revolutionise home lives and the field of entertainment.' It did!

I think that Jay should have the last word. 'Some of that life has survived. Much has gone for good: gypsies going on foot from village to village, door to door, telling fortunes and asking for silver to cross their palms, travelling tinsmiths and knife sharpeners, the fisherman who cycled, or walked, miles to sell his catch, barefoot children haunting the misery of the weekly Belfast cattle market. We see fewer mice in our houses and rats in our gardens and yards, but they are still not far away, but we will do what we have always done, just get on with it.'

Tom Crocker. (Photograph by Bill Henry)

Bibliography

Allan, Harry, *Donaghadee: an Illustrated History*, The White Row Press, 2006.

Bates, Nora, *Up the Down Street*, Adare Press, 1994.

Barton, Brian, *The Belfast Blitz*, Belfast Historical Foundation, 2015.

Bell, Jonathan and Mervyn Watson, *Farming in Ulster*, Friars Bush Press, 1988.

Bellaghy Historical Society, *Life in the Past*, private publication, 2005.

Doherty, James, *Post 381, Memoirs of a Belfast Air Raid Warden,* Friars Bush Press, 1989.

Douds, Stephen, *The Belfast Blitz, the People's Story*, Blackstaff Press, 2011.

Dolan, Kevin, Hon. President Cuchulainn Cycling Club (ed.), *Dundalk A Cycling History 1819–2010,* private publication, 2010.

Galway, James, *An Autobiography*, Chapell & Company Ltd, 1978.

Kilpatrick, Noel, *In the Shadows of the Gantries*, Alcon Press, 1992.

McBride, Doreen (ed.), *Great Verse to Stand Up and Tell Them,* Adare Press, 1996.

McBride, Doreen, *What They Did With Plants,* Adare Press, 1991.

McClure, Elaine, *Bodies in Our Back Yard*, Ulster Society (Publications) Ltd, 1994.

Quinn, Patsy, *Dear Little Town*, private publication, supported by Newry and Mourne Cultural Arts Committee, 2006.

Taylor, Marilyn, *Faraway Home*, O'Brien Press, 1999.

Skuce, Dolly, *Magic Lanterns to Moon Landings,* Adare Press, 1995.

Bradley, Patience, *Where Did You Go My Lovely*, Excalibur Press, 2017.
This book gives an insight into the glamorous world of dancers who appeared on television. Patience danced with Legs and Co. and became a top model for *Vogue* magazine during the 1980s, so strictly speaking it is outside the remit *of We Just Got on With it*